TWELVE STEPS AND TWELVE TRADITIONS

of GreySheeters Anonymous

TWELVE STEPS AND TWELVE TRADITIONS

of GreySheeters Anonymous

October, 2015

Library of Congress Control Number: 2015916118

ISBN:	Hardcover	978-1-5144-1269-5
	Softcover	978-1-5144-1270-1
	eBook	978-1-5144-1268-8

This is GreySheeters Anonymous World Services Conference-Approved Literature.

In an effort to combat the overwhelming challenges of food addiction, a group decision from the GreySheet community was made to release this first edition of the GreySheeters Twelve Steps and Twelve Traditions to show support for the still sick and suffering food addict. All stories are original and submitted with their authors' full permission. This book is not a replacement, it is an addition.

Print information available on the last page.

Rev. date: 11/05/2015

To order additional copies of this book, contact:
Xlibris
1-888-795-4274
www.Xlibris.com
Orders@Xlibris.com
549369

TABLE OF CONTENTS

This first edition of *Twelve Steps and Twelve Traditions of GreySheeters Anonymous* is dedicated to the pioneers who worked tirelessly to bring us here. Their dedication, hard work and vision gave us: ownership of the GreySheet; development of a World Services Board; the guidance to build GreySheeters Anonymous intergroups, and so much more.

Pioneers, you are appreciated and treasured.

Thank You

INTRODUCTION

Welcome to the first edition of the Twelve Steps and Twelve Traditions of GreySheeters Anonymous.

GreySheeters Anonymous (GSA) is a fellowship of individuals who are collectively solving our eating problems. GSA has helped people who have tried but previously failed to gain lasting freedom from being controlled by food. We do not offer another diet! It is an abstinence program for compulsive eaters and food addicts. For us, the GreySheet is a specific food plan that takes away cravings for grains, sugar, and alcohol.

GSA offers a clearly defined abstinence (our definition of sobriety from food addiction), proven tools, and support from a worldwide community. In GSA people share personal experience, strength, and hope to help each other recover from compulsive behaviors around food. There are no dues or fees. We are self-supporting through our contributions. We are not aligned with any other group or organization.

If you think you might be one of us, join us. Attend at least six meetings and consider if you identify with the physical, mental, emotional, and spiritual aspects of the disease and recovery. Get a sponsor, try our program, and stay long enough to experience for yourself the freedoms that come as a result of doing this program one day at a time consecutively. You will be amazed.

THE TWELVE STEPS AND TWELVE TRADITIONS OF GREYSHEETERS ANONYMOUS

This text is a resource for GreySheeters---a book filled with Experience, Strength, and Hope (ESH) specific to food addiction, compulsive eating, overeating, or under eating. This text is for those who use the GreySheeters Anonymous recovery program and the GreySheet food plan. Others are certainly welcome to use this text; however, be forewarned that the frequent references to the GreySheet and the GreySheet Steps and Traditions may create a yearning for abstinence which only a sponsor in GSA and use of the GreySheet food plan will satisfy. The GreySheet comes with a sponsor. The tools that a sponsor and sponsee share offer GreySheet abstinence and recovery.

These are suggested readings used for regular meetings, retreats, A Way of Life (AWOL) groups, or with a sponsor or trusted adviser. We work together one on one or in a group. We meet face to face or on phone conference calls. Many also use online communication methods.

The best way to work the steps is with a step sponsor who has worked through them and can serve as a guide to share personal experiences. Using the same process with the Traditions and a service sponsor, a wiser member who has done service in groups and service beyond the group level, opens new doors. The food, step, and service sponsors may be the same person or different ones. Each sponsor shares his or her personal experience, strength, and hope, regarding food, steps, and service.

Some ask when is the best time to work the Steps and Traditions? Talk with your sponsor and listen to what is shared. Some start doing steps after reaching 90 days of abstinence. Others begin with step one at the beginning of their recovery. If you are having difficulty getting abstinent, taking a first step will help you surrender. If you are reading this, the best time may be right now.

Working the traditions often follows the recovery of step work. The Traditions focus on relationships. This work may be needed sooner rather than later. The Traditions apply to our GSA groups as well as families and relationships in work settings.

The GSA Steps and Traditions are also the basis for closed group meetings and sharing in AWOL groups that meet and work through the material together. The friendships created in these closed groups often remove the isolation of years of compulsive eating and food addiction. We are not alone. We hear the experience, strength, and hope shared.

One group meets face to face monthly in a mini-marathon meeting with people frequently traveling an hour and a half. They read the step of the month, answer the questions, and then hear a member qualify for 20 minutes with a focus on that step, and finally, share in an open forum.

After the two-hour meeting, people enjoy a potluck meal and do steps with newcomers to share their experience of staying abstinent in GreySheeters Anonymous.

Another group gets together quarterly from several states to share a meal and participate in meetings. Outpost loners, GreySheeters that live in an area where there are no other GreySheeters, need not be alone.

AWOLs have met on the phone using versions of these Steps. Participants have benefitted from identification, not only with the disease, food addiction, and compulsive eating but also with our unique solution - use of the GreySheet food plan, Steps, and Traditions.

AWOLs are not GSA meetings or GSA groups. They have their unique agreements for participation, leadership, and membership. We listen carefully to the expectations, books to be used, prerequisites, and agreements prior to taking the commitment to participate in an AWOL. GSA AWOLs enlist membership from around the world, and as a result, friendships have blossomed into close relationships.

Working the Steps multiple times brings new insights for action, service, and personal growth. Reflections on the principles of this book change over time. Thus learning to prosper in life and service with our Traditions allows us to grow in usefulness.

We hope that you find this book helpful for yourself and those you sponsor. Ours is a one day at a time program of recovery from a progressive and fatal disease. We wish you physical, mental, emotional, and spiritual recovery.

The main goal of working these GreySheeters Anonymous Steps and Traditions is to obtain and maintain abstinence from compulsive eating and active food addiction and to help other compulsive eaters and food addicts who still suffer. We have the opportunity to live new lives with the freedoms gained from our insights, recovery, and new relationships with others and God, *as we understand Him*.

THE DOCTOR'S EXPERIENCE

My name is Dr. Vera Tarman. I am the Medical Director of a major treatment center in Toronto. I have treated over five thousand people suffering from alcohol and drugs. Over the course of years, I have noticed that many of my patients have in common a history of disordered eating patterns. They either had an eating disorder prior to their current addiction, or they developed an eating disorder while in recovery from their substance of abuse.

There were the patients who compulsively overate as children, later to become alcoholics. There was the anorexic that 'cured' her disease when she found that cocaine was more appealing. There was the addict who substituted a continuous intake of sugar to satisfy his cravings for drugs. Many found that their past eating disorder returned once they put down their drink or drug. Sometimes this led to purging or a return to drug use to maintain weight control.

It became apparent to me that there was a common feature amongst many of these patients. Each continued to show an obsession of the mind and the compulsive use of a substance to manage moods. I could not help but conclude that the disease of addiction must include food as a substance of abuse, along with drugs and alcohol.

I then decided to observe people in the general population who were diagnosed with disordered eating patterns. I discovered that there were people who eat in ways very similar to those alcoholics and drug addicts that I have treated. These are people who might have had *no other addiction.* Some of these people display the same features Addiction Doctors use to diagnose addictions.

These individuals have developed cravings for specific foods, perhaps choosing favorites over healthier foods. They obsess about particular foods, typically those high in sugar, the way an alcoholic will obsess about the next drink. Some are *grazers*, constantly eating to manage the distressing feelings that would otherwise break through. Others are *binge eaters,* seeking out large quantities of food to feel happy, elated, or just to numb their emotional pain. Daily work or leisure routines could be disrupted since binges and purges can last a whole day. In general, these people spend a good portion of the day obsessing about food, either through eating or restricting, or recovering from the effects of too much or too little food.

Soon enough, many will develop a craving for specific foods, needing more to get the same feeling of comfort or numbness or satisfaction. Typically, withdrawal symptoms of irritability, anxiety, even insomnia, or physical pain occur if the individuals do not succumb to their food cravings. People frequently start off with the intention to have only a 'few' and then find that they eat the whole thing, unable to stop at the promised first few bites or taste. Just one was never enough. It was also common to see people continue to eat problematically, despite the ill consequences. No matter how ill they became, the problematic eating did not stop. I observe that people frequently isolate, allowing their social circles to narrow down to only a few people who share or tolerate their obsession.

When these people have tried to stop their disordered eating, they might resist for a few days to a few weeks, only to succumb to unmanageable eating once again. Their obsession about food is continuous, regardless of whether they are restricting or overeating. This lack of control usually leads to remorse, anxiety, depression, self-loathing, and a progressive worsening of the symptoms. These are the *hallmark signs* of addiction. I have found individuals who fit these criteria through all walks of life, such as compulsive overeater, food addict, or under-eater in diet programs, eating disorder programs, etc. All share in common a heightened sensitivity to food and eating behavior. Once they have the first bite, despite attempts to hold back, they find they are unable to control their food intake after that.

What are the reasons for this aberrant eating behavior? I have looked to the research and have discovered that there is a high association between users of drugs and alcohol and those with eating disorders. When we look at the science of addiction, and the emerging neuroimaging technology, such as functional MRIs, and SPECT scans, we can see a similar neural dynamic to that of the addictive behavior surrounding drugs and alcohol.

Behaviors, healthy or unhealthy, are connected to the same pool of neurochemicals. The neurochemicals, such as dopamine, serotonin, and endorphins, travel particular neural pathways to influence our moods, giving feelings of safety, comfort, joy, elation. It is by virtue of replicating or mimicking these neurochemicals; that particular foods can produce the same effect as a drug.

Specific foods such as sugar share the same neurochemistry and neural pathways as cocaine. Foods such as sweetened chocolate do even more so, as these mimic alcohol and opiate effects. These foods act as mood modulators and pain anesthetizers and can be as effective as many drugs. Specific foods and even large quantities of food substitute for drugs. If persons have a heightened sensitivity or allergic response to a particular food, they will have a greater response to that food than the person who does not and who may eat that food with impunity. This heightened sensitivity may be due to genetics. As we have determined with alcoholism, it is apparent that there is a *strong family history* of people suffering from eating disorders. Studies on obesity have shown there is an association between weight, problematic eating practices, and a neurochemical imbalance that leads to depression. The afflicted individuals will *'self-medicate'* their mood disorder with food.

An *obsession of the mind* is triggered by the quantity of the food itself. If eaten in large quantities, even healthy foods, such as green vegetables, can trigger a *binge cycle*. The health advocate who is grazing or bingeing on 'healthy' foods throughout the day may demonstrate a response to the overabundance of particular foods. For example, notice the orange skin of someone eating lots of carrots and squash. One may be getting malnourished from the lack of another vital food. This behavior overwhelms the body's checks and balances to curb appetite, digestion, and metabolism. The body needs to digest a certain amount of food a day to maintain a workable balance. Balance is jarred by uneven amounts, whether the food is energy dense, such as sugars, or is less energy dense, such as vegetables. The vulnerable Food Addict appears to be especially dependent on maintaining an ideal balance of quantity.

The problem for the compulsive overeater, food addict or under-eater is a physical craving that starts once the person has had the first bite. The emotional, non-rational brain is triggered, and the rational mind of the compulsive overeater, food addict, or under-eater is transformed into one characterized by *obsessive thinking and compulsive behavior.*

One treatment is the promotion of complete abstinence from the problematic drug. It would follow that the treatment for food addiction is an avoidance of specific foods. A compulsive overeater, food addict or under-eater will balk and say "You can stop drugs, but you can't stop eating!"

True. The clear instruction is the avoidance of designated foods, such as sugar and its close cousin on the glycemic index, grain. My experience has shown that restraint may be needed to cover a broad spectrum of foods since any food can eventually become a trigger to the compulsive mind. Once it has become so, it too must be avoided. Eating behaviors that upset the compulsive overeater's, food addict's or under-eater's precarious natural balance, such as the over or under consumption of food, or the consumption of food which triggers cravings, must also be avoided.

The general medical consensus in most programs, especially eating disorder programs, tends to be to teach the individual to eat all foods in prescribed amounts. This is akin to the harm reduction treatment plan or the popular "controlled or moderate" drinking solution sometimes recommended for the treatment of alcoholism, in contrast with the recommendation of complete abstinence. This approach is doomed for food addicts and reawakens the mental obsession and the physical cravings and the actions that we define as relapse.

Is the avoidance of specific foods alone a sufficient solution? While helpful on the level of physical health, these restrictions may not be a sufficient response in maintaining long-term success. Like the 'dry drunks,' alcoholics who are not 'working a Twelve Step program,' food addicts must find a way to live contentedly without their desired drug of choice. Restricting certain foods alone does not appear to be enough for the long term. If we are to look for programs of successful recovery and sobriety, we can conclude that recovery from food addiction will require a mental and a spiritual solution, alongside a physical program of maintaining food abstentions.

The Twelve Step program addresses just this. We addiction clinicians have seen the growth and strength of these programs. We have seen how valuable fellowship, guidance from a sponsor, and a spiritual program are to filling in the 'holes' that the drug and using behavior addressed. However, most of these fellowships do not support a firm adherence to the principle of specific food restrictions.

There is one Twelve Step group called GreySheeters Anonymous or GSA that does. While there are other peer groups that focus on habitual overeating and other disordered eating patterns, this group has uniquely promoted avoidance of specific foods and food behaviors. This group targets the needs of the compulsive overeater, food addict, or under-eater.

I urge you to listen to the stories of individual members. You will hear that recovery from food addiction is possible, both in the immediate and long term. These individuals have discovered on their own, through trial and error, the imperative of specific food restrictions, called food "abstinence."

They have now created a community to support and sustain their recovery. In addition to food 'sobriety,' called 'back-to-back abstinence,' they have found it necessary to apply a spiritual solution to their disorder.

The various techniques, such as frequent meetings, abstinence, and the daily phone/email support along with rigorous sponsorship are some of the common tools. Working the program of abstinence and the twelve steps, traditions, and concepts of GreySheeters Anonymous are essential for lifelong recovery. I believe that this understanding of grain, sugar, and other food addictions, as substances of abuse, makes this group ideal for the compulsive overeater, food addict, or under-eater. I encourage people struggling with problematic eating behaviors to listen to these stories and to practice these Steps and Traditions to see if they qualify as a compulsive overeater, food addict, or under-eater. If they do qualify, I recommend this approach as sound and very likely to help achieve clarity of mind and the freedom from the obsession with food and the phenomenon of craving.

Dr. Vera Tarman

GreySheeters Anonymous
TWELVE STEPS

Step One: We admitted we were powerless over food - that our lives had become unmanageable.

We came to GreySheeters Anonymous (GSA) from all walks of life to find freedom from the food and substance cravings that once ruled us. We have been relieved from compulsive eating and its consequences. We are free of the masks we wore to cover our shame and guilt. The negative self-talk that once ruled us, no matter where we were or what we were doing, began to disappear.

Every member of GSA has an unusual relationship with food. When *in the food,* what we call being under the influence of food, we experience mood swings and withdrawal. We also misinterpret the behaviors of others. All of this means sinking deeper into the swamp of despair.

We were anorexic or bulimic, exercised to excess, or used diuretics and laxatives to control the physical effects of eating. We watched in hopeless anguish as the numbers on the scale began to reflect the changes in our bodies. For others, the scale at home could no longer record the weight we had gained. We alternated between eating recklessly and then stretches of iron-fisted, white-knuckled willpower with perfect adherence to commercial weight-loss diet and exercise plans. Our attempts eventually ended in failure with a return to compulsive eating and additional weight gain. When every hope for a spiritual, emotional, or physical solution was lost, we finally gave up hope. This was the surrender that preceded Step One.

We came to GSA knowing this was the "last house on the block," meaning our last hope after countless attempts at permanent weight control. We had feelings of desperation that only the dying have felt. Could we accept the consequences of our behaviors? We were powerless over our compulsive eating and cravings, yet in GSA we found a path to freedom. Some said, "It's the food, the food, the food." This seemed too simple at first, but when we followed their actions, we found for ourselves that complete abstinence from specific food items, combined with working the steps, was the solution to our problem.

For the first time, we acknowledged that we were sensitive to grains and sugars. Some said we had developed allergies to these substances. Some GSA members agree that ours is a program for those who have an allergy or sensitivity to grains and sugars. By following this program, which includes eating three weighed and measured meals a day from the GreySheet food plan, we have a reprieve from an eating disorder that brought us to hopelessness and close to death. We came to a new awareness of how our disease manifested. We were victims of its physical ravages and the subsequent thoughts we believed as truth. Freedom from the consequences of compulsive eating was worth whatever actions the GSA program suggested we take.

Some struggled for decades, unwilling or unable to surrender the foods that were killing us. Our cultures sometimes encouraged consumption of food items that our bodies could not tolerate. Once certain foods were eaten, the phenomenon of craving was initiated. Our emotions repeatedly led us to self-loathing, disgust, and despair. We felt humiliated and hopeless and often hated ourselves. These feelings clashed with interpersonal relations in our families, with co-workers in our work settings, and with others as we ate our way to the mortuary.

We of GSA became willing to admit defeat. What did we need to do to have this horrible compulsion eliminated? Hopeless and helpless, we became willing to surrender our beliefs, attitudes, and experiences with food. We agreed to commit our food for the next 24 hours to a qualified GSA food sponsor. We define this as someone with 90 days or more of back to back abstinence on the GreySheet. This new surrender signaled our acceptance of the program. A one-day-at-a-time commitment was made. This commitment was the beginning of the first step.

The second part of the first step is equally important. We admitted that our lives had become unmanageable.

For some of us, unmanageability was more evident than the powerlessness of the first step. To witness the mess of a compulsive eater's car, desk, or bedroom floor is to observe the unmanageable aspect of the disease. The places where we ate proved that our eating was out of control. Many of us had careers that were affected by our repeated warfare with food. The emotional mood swings decimated hopes for advancement and accolades.

Some who had wanted to marry or commit to a long-term relationship instead were in the grips of compulsive eating. The eating took the form of angry outbursts, depression, and misplaced anxieties that limited the ability to be a caring, responsible partner. Some of us were not able to have children because of health issues related to our eating histories. Our attitudes, behaviors, and outbursts clearly harmed the people closest to us.

Nonetheless, some of us had great successes, but at the cost of our mental health. Anguish filled every waking moment with shame and guilt. Fear and terror ruled every night. We hid our compulsive behaviors from the world. We carried great burdens in emotional weight that resulted in a loss of self-respect and personal creativity.

We found that we gained peace when our "unmanageability" was diminished. As the Twelve Steps were taken, in conjunction with a committed food plan, growth occurred on all three levels: emotional, spiritual, and physical.

Some of us came to the fellowship at a normal weight, yet burdened by the phenomenon of craving, unable to stop after the first bite. The GSA program helped these individuals as well. They too were freed from the cravings and granted a clear enough mind to stay abstinent and be of service to other compulsive eaters.

The most common reason for returning to compulsive eating is a failure to understand that unmanageability continues, one day at a time. The freedom and release that come from working the Twelve Steps are lost if our powerlessness over compulsive eating is questioned. We have found that it is only by following this Twelve Step path that we were able to experience more clarity of mind. When one of us becomes convinced that she or he can remain sane while eating grains and sugars, the concept of Step One is defeated. On a daily basis, each of us must continue to acknowledge powerlessness over food and life's unmanageability. Only in this way has abstinence been possible.

We struggled repeatedly to find a way to eat like normal people but have found our bodies and minds are different. We have a disease. To beat this, we commit to our program for one day. For us, it is too difficult to live in the future or to try to repair the years past. Instead, we think in terms of one day and surrender our committed food accordingly. Only by surrendering do we find a solution. Abstinence precedes and then supports recovery one day at a time in GSA.

Personal Step One Experiences

Freedom from the Phenomenon of Craving

In the early 1970's, I came to a Twelve Step program for food, and the GreySheet plan was placed in my hands. It worked. I lost excess pounds but subsequently made the decision to try a 'normal' eating regime and gained my weight back. In the 1980's, I went to a different Twelve Step program for food and once again lost weight using the GreySheet. However, as soon as I began to add specific food items, regardless of the quantity, the phenomenon of craving returned. I would weep after breakfast every morning because I could not add to the meal more of the foods that I craved. I lost weight, but I struggled to maintain the weight loss. When I encountered a difference of opinion regarding definitions of abstinence within the fellowship, I became resentful and left.

Alone and afraid, I gained one hundred pounds over the next eight years. In 1998, I attended my first GreySheeters Anonymous meeting. I got a GSA sponsor and committed my next meal to her. That was the beginning of the journey that brought me to today's abstinence, which has lasted seventeen continuous years, the longest in my life. I have discovered that my 'eyeballing it' gauge is broken. By weighing and measuring my food, I do not have to guess what is considered 'enough.' I do not consume grains, sugars, or alcohol. This means I do not develop the phenomenon of craving for more. I no longer have aching joints or clouded, confused thinking. I am a compulsive eater and food addict in recovery. I commit my meals to my sponsor or another GSA member who has achieved at least ninety days of abstinence. I do not eat between meals no matter what. My abstinence and sobriety are the most important things in my life today. It is only with abstinence and sobriety that I have a Higher Power, a loving husband, a home, creativity, service opportunities, and self-respect. I surrender to the GSA program and my Higher Power each day. As a result, everything in my life has changed. I am so grateful to be abstinent!

Powerless

I remember, sometimes multiple times daily, that I am powerless over compulsive eating and the lure of sweets and carbohydrates. The consequences of indulging are devastating to my self-worth and desire to live. When I relapsed, I crossed the line. I tried and could not get back for eight years. I could not trust myself to get through breakfast abstinently. My work meant nothing. Once I started eating, I could not stop and didn't want to. I have to remember that I was enslaved to food every waking hour. I have to remember that the illusion of enjoying sweets and carbohydrates is just that – an illusion. Telling myself that I will eat delicious food is a lie. When I relapsed, I ate tasteless bags of food. Nothing was good. I went for the junk because I couldn't wait to prepare delicious food. Today I have to do grocery shopping that is still not my favorite task. I know that if I do not shop and keep myself supplied with abstinent food, I am in danger of discarding it all to go back to compulsively eating. Admitting that I am powerless over food reminds me daily of the dire consequences if I were to choose to no longer be abstinent.

Addicted- How Do I Remember?

It was very hard for me to accept that I have an addiction and that it is incurable. I need to keep in my mind every day how powerless I am over the food and how I felt reaching the bottom. My disease is very easy to forget. I need to refresh the feeling of powerlessness regularly and one of the possibilities to do this is answering questions on Step One. It is an ongoing step. I can also remember when I share with another. I need GSA one day at a time because I am powerless over food.

Life Beyond My Dreams

When I came to GSA there was no doubt in my mind that I was powerless over food and that my life had become unmanageable. This was not always so. I had taken my son to see the psychologist, but she sent my son home and kept me. The psychologist suggested that I go to a 12 Step Program for food. I rebelled. I remember saying, "I don't need a program. I have a job where I direct people and tell them what to do." It was that attitude that kept me away from recovery for years. I finally ended up in a food program that worked perfectly until I added the allowed grains. Eventually beaten and broken I was willing to admit my powerlessness and crawled into the rooms of GSA.

The meaning of this step is my admission that I'm TOTALLY powerless over food, and I am a compulsive eater through and through. That's the way I'm wired. I will never be able to eat "normally." I have physical allergies and an addiction to food, and my brain does not register when I have enough. I have a disease of "more." I was born this way.

In the past, I tried all kinds of diets. I used to be triggered by all of the things we do not eat in GSA. Once I start eating those foods, I unleashed the food monster inside of me, I could never stop until I was physically sick, and my head would become heavy and numb. Alcoholics describe this condition as a blackout.

I also tried to "outsmart" my program, 'doing GreySheet with exception.' I was weighing and measuring all my food but also allowed myself to have certain foods that were not a part of GSA. Justifying that these foods were good for me, that I was not as sick as other people in the program, and that I could control my food on my own. The result was horrible: I ate more, felt dishonest, was not at peace, gained weight, and hated myself. On my own I can't have a healthy relationship with food. Period. I need my GreySheet fellowship, phone meetings, a sponsor, all of the tools of the program, God, and God's power to relieve me of this bondage to food. I know today that only by weighing and measuring my food using the GreySheet food plan can I have peace around food, serenity, health, a slender and fit body, and a life beyond my wildest dreams.

HOPE

Many of us have shared and cited real life examples. I too am powerless over food. Using my power to control my life and the food is not a fight I can win. My energies are available to use elsewhere today. I'm no longer tied to trying to control the food. I know and understand that my life was not working. I surrender to this program and what it requires of me to stay abstinent and get my life back. Here in "the rooms," I am living a Twelve Step life, one day at a time: calling my sponsor, weighing and measuring my food from the GreySheet food plan without exception, participating in meetings, working with others in the program, and working on my recovery. I finally can feel myself getting healthier. When I see progress, I feel hope. Now, instead of being caught up in a vicious cycle, I'm on the road of recovery, always moving forward. I can connect with a God of my understanding, and I can feel good about my life. I'm at peace with the world and myself.

Step One

After completing all the questions for Step One, I realized I had gone too quickly. Listening each week to our members in the AWOL (A Way of Life) group helped me to see the things I had left out. In Step One I acknowledge that I am powerless over food, and it generates in me the understanding that just like alcohol, sugar and grain create a craving that I cannot control. Finally what a relief it is to understand that. I always beat myself for not being able to stop eating. Now I understand. Like alcoholism, my food addiction is unmanageable by me. If I take one bite, it is over. I am so grateful to the GSA program because it has put the puzzle together for me that previously always had missing pieces. Even in sobriety my life was unmanageable because I was in the food. GreySheeters Anonymous abstinence makes my life with food livable. Maintaining GSA abstinence is the most important thing that God and I can do. Without God, I could never have put the food down.

Men Suffer Too

I had always been chubby, and the food was my master from an early age. In late adolescence, the loneliness of being a 19-year-old virgin would make drugs and alcohol alluring. I was so thirsty for something greater than myself; this program has quenched that.

I was 12 stepped into GreySheeters Anonymous by a sponsor from another program. He had been abstinent for six years back to back, but I wasn't ready. I left that meeting with a GreySheet, a sponsor, and a commitment of what to eat for lunch and dinner. But the action of buying a scale was lost to the call of the drive through windows. A year later, three years clean and sober, miserable and morbidly obese, I was ready, I thought. After a week of abstinence, I left for a trip to New Orleans, and I wasn't ready to travel so early in abstinence. I got my first case of the "screw-its" and destroyed myself for the remainder of the trip. Hurricane Katrina, which followed our leaving by a day or so, was a suitable metaphor for what I had done to my body for my entire life until then.

I got abstinent a few days after returning to my local community. A kindly man told me words I never forgot. He said, "You have to take this program more seriously...." I got involved in the fellowship and did service, but secretly I had a reservation. The program works, as does the food plan, and over the next two years, I released 160 pounds. However, like I've heard so many say, at the end of that somewhat self-obsessed process, I started to believe that *I* had lost all that weight. After two years and a month, I started to listen to the snake-like voice that said, "You don't need to do this anymore. You know what to do and plus, *she* doesn't like the planning, the protecting, and the lack of spontaneity...."

Ironically, after a year of controlled eating and compulsive exercise, I came back to GreySheet after *she* was no longer in the picture! I was a few sizes higher, but still unconvinced that I was powerless over food. For the next five years, I would gravitate towards GreySheet every time life got too difficult, but I wasn't willing to concede that I was licked. I treated this 12 step program as a diet club, so when I left with another one of my reservations, I got bigger and bigger.

Finally after a disastrous move to another part of the country and another relationship that fueled my compulsive eating - this woman was a *baker* - the one thing that had never occurred to me in GreySheeters Anonymous happened. Despite having been in other 12 step programs and being very successful in them, *I,* without even realizing it had a first step experience in GreySheeters Anonymous. It happened on a sunny Saturday when I opened a package from a national retailer, and in the package were clothing sizes that were as big as what I wore before I came into GSA. In the end, after years of starts and stops, controlled eating, bingeing, compulsive exercise, all sorts of other diets and even other 12 step programs, I had finally gained every single pound back.

It took a few more weeks and a move back to my familiar environs, but I was finally willing to make GreySheet abstinence the most important thing in my life and my primary purpose. I now do all the things that I was never willing to do, the things the long-timers do. Since returning I have released over 100 pounds again, for the fourth or fifth time, and I live my life doing the actions that ensure my abstinence. I am creating an insurance policy, and I will never again, one day at a time, allow the mind that had me convinced that treating my body like this was a reasonable idea. I pray the men I sponsor will not make all the mistakes I have made in my journey, so I love to work with chronic relapsers just like me. GreySheeters Anonymous is an incredible way of life. I hope you find what you seek here, and you stay to pass it on!

Step One Questions:

1. Before GSA, how was I powerless over compulsive eating and food addiction?
2. How does my powerlessness show up now that I am a member of the program?
3. What did admitting that I am powerless over compulsive eating mean when getting abstinent? What does it mean to me today?
4. How was my life unmanageable before the program?
5. What does unmanageability mean to me today?
6. On my own, can I accept that I cannot control my eating?
7. How does the admission of powerlessness and unmanageability prepare me for the rest of the Steps?
8. In what ways have I tried to convince myself and others that my eating was manageable? What were the consequences?
9. Do I believe that by working Step One, my eating will become manageable? If not, why not?
10. What might happen if I surrendered and accepted that I am bodily and mentally different from others who do not share my food addiction and compulsive eating disease?
11. Have I tried "quick fix" solutions offered by the different kinds of media? What were the outcomes?
12. What has been the result of thinking that somehow, someday I will be able to eat 'normally?'
13. How have I experienced shame or embarrassment related to my compulsive eating? What were the results?
14. Now that I am abstinent, what have I experienced in terms of shame and embarrassment? How have I addressed these feelings or experiences? What have been the outcomes?
15. How might I change my outlook and release any shame or embarrassment around weighing and measuring my food in public?
16. What brought me to GSA? What did I hope to find here? What have I learned?
17. In what ways has my thinking changed since coming to GSA?
18. What do I want in GSA recovery?
19. Who expressed concern for my health prior to my coming to GSA? What did they say?

20. How have friends and family reacted to my acceptance of the GSA program? How have I addressed their reactions? What responses have been the most effective?
21. Now that I am a GSA member, in what ways do I feel differently about myself?
22. Do I need the approval of others to continue this program one day at a time?
23. In what ways do I take care of myself today? How can I continue to take care of myself?
24. In what new ways do I say 'Yes' and 'No' today? In what ways can I practice new behaviors?
25. When my meal planning and preparation go smoothly, what do I tell myself today?
26. When and how have I been challenged to commit to the GSA program? How did I respond? What were the outcomes?
27. HALT (Hungry, Angry, Lonely, and Tired) is an acronym that many in Twelve Step programs use; some members prefer HALT SF (Hungry, Angry, Lonely, Tired, Serious, and Fabulous.) The acronym encourages members to stop and take note of one's personal condition. How does this apply in GSA?
28. Now that I am in GSA, how do I respond differently to thirst, anxiety, fogginess, and discontent?
29. What specific feelings challenge me the most? What ways have I found to address these challenges?
30. When I find myself struggling, what can I do or think to bring relief? What tools do I have to assist me?
31. What slogans have I learned that support my GSA program?
32. When life is going smoothly, or I have celebrations, what do I need to remember?
33. How do I know that I have surrendered to Step One in GSA?

Step Two: Came to believe that a Power greater than ourselves could restore us to sanity.

Recovering compulsive eaters say, "We came. We came to. We came to believe." This is true for those of us who had come to the program foggy from the effects of the sugar we had been eating. Many of those foods are used to manufacture alcohol. Had our bodies somehow converted the grains and sugars we were eating into mind-altering substances? Many newcomers struggle with the basic mathematics we use to weigh and measure our food. Many remark with astonishment at the clarity, which comes soon after beginning the program. Are these indicators of the "came" and "came to" parts of this step? Yes, we think so.

The concept, "came to believe," is hard to understand for some. No one comes to GSA who hasn't struggled with food challenges. We had become hopeless or had accepted, "This is just the way I am." One GSA member wore a straitjacket when she went to bed to control her nighttime eating binges. Ultimately, abstinence and prayer were solutions.

How did we come to believe that there is another way? How did we surrender to a belief? One compulsive eater was told to get on her knees and pray. Some use the acronym PUSH: Pray until something happens.

One woman, when asked by her sponsor if she believed that her Higher Power had control over her desire to eat, responded with a rousing, "No! If God could have helped during my years of suffering, why hadn't the result been different?"

To this the sponsor replied, "We came, came to, and then came to believe. Keep coming back. Listen in meetings. Continue to surrender your food choices by committing your food to your sponsor and weigh and measure each meal. You too, as so many of us have, will experience changes in your beliefs."

For those who have come to the program with religious training, we invite you to review your personal beliefs. While the doubts described above may not apply, this step may still require a deeper surrender where food is concerned. What does this mean? "Yes, I already have faith that works in my life, but it hasn't helped me with the food."

One long timer commented, "Surrender to a Power greater than myself meant that this Power could restore me to sanity *even with the food.* I still need to surrender further, if I have not yet come to believe that a Power greater than myself could restore me to sanity." Abstinence from grains and sugars with weighed and measured meals in GSA is the sanest behavior we can initially demonstrate. Over time, abstinence often includes other behaviors as well.

Newcomers and long-timers come to accept a Higher Power in a variety of ways. Some find within themselves a desire to go deeper into their existing faiths. Others remove the "No Trespassing" sign put up to protect their intimate relationship with food. Then they find that it is not the Power greater than themselves that has been missing. Rather it had been a lack of openness to that Power that had prevented them from being restored to sanity: Willingness proved to be the answer. Others take the GSA group as a Power greater than themselves because the group demonstrates sanity that the individual may not yet experience. Some newcomers decide to take the group as a higher power, which translates the program and passes on what has been learned in GSA. Whatever way we find a Power greater than ourselves that can restore us to sanity, we can work this Step. As we grow and change, most come to a different experience of that Power.

One member described her frustration at repeatedly returning to doing it "my way." Each return to compulsive eating was more painful and harmful than the last. Nevertheless, she kept coming to meetings. Again, in desperation, she cried out, "I just can't get it."

A long-timer responded, "You can have abstinence if you want it, and if you are willing to do what we do, and then do it." She was right.

Willingness has been described as the key that opens the door to recovery. Once through the door, beginning steps include surrendering the food to a sponsor and a Higher Power. The path becomes clearer as we weigh and measure our food and eat only what we have committed and nothing in between. With our sponsor's guidance and the GSA Steps, Traditions, and Concepts, a spiritual road of sanity opens before us.

How does this newfound sanity first appear? First, we abstain from compulsive eating and active food addiction one day at the time. Some members feel as though everyday life is easier because there are fewer obstacles to overcome. Maybe the same obstacles are there, but they do not seem as irritating or impossible. Ways around troublesome events appear out of thin air. Words come to mind to deal with situations in a sane manner. Some don't feel that their lives are easier, but they continue to do what they need to do to stay abstinent.

The sanity of mind can be as simple as acceptance of what *is*, as opposed to living in denial, which is not seeing *reality as it is*. A sane body is the absence of food cravings. One benefit is that healthy responses come from an abstinent body and mind. Another benefit is the ability to consider the impact of our actions. For brief moments, we are in the flow. One member described it as: "I am in alignment with my Higher Power. Everything is exactly as it should be at this moment. My heart is at peace."

Sometimes we can see sanity more clearly when we have slipped off the path and have returned to old behaviors. We see the contrast. A definition of insanity is doing the same thing over and over and expecting a different result. The clarity of mind that comes with GSA abstinence increases with time. It allows us to discard our blinders that kept us in our self-obsessed world, personalizing everything, and over-reacting to the behavior of others. "She's having a bad day" was what 'they' said about us, but now we can recognize that 'they' have bad days too. We no longer take their bad days personally. We can demonstrate more tolerance for ourselves and others.

The self-pitying question, "Why me?" and constant victim like thinking must be let go. We no longer played the 'blame game' or needed to continue in the triangular drama of assigning or assuming the victim, rescuer, and perpetrator roles. Freedom is available. With our dignity restored, we can walk the path of recovery called abstinence.

By maintaining physical abstinence one day at a time, each of us 'came, came to, and then came to believe' in a Power greater than ourselves. Many of us concluded that this Higher Power *could* restore us to the sanity of mind and body. The cravings, which ruled us, disappeared. We discover this is enough. One member concludes her daily writing: "I am enough. It is enough. I live in an abundant universe. All is well."

We came for the vanity and stayed for the sanity. Clarity of mind and spirituality are the gifts to which we refer when we say, "I gained so much more than a right-sized body." Step Three expands on this.

Personal Step Two Experiences

The Ongoing Search

On my own I am insane regarding many things, especially around food. If I want to develop some sanity in my life, I need help. I need help stronger than my insanity! I also need to recover from my eating disorder. This help comes from the fellowship and a relationship with my Higher Power.

When I arrived in GSA I believed that only a Power greater than I could restore to me the sanity I needed and craved. By then I had tried all methods humanly possible. When I joined GSA, I was hoping for a better, closer relationship with this Power. I thought it might happen. I was delightfully surprised when I lost weight. As I have progressed, I believe that I have grown closer to this great Power. I still think I have a long way to go. Hopefully, this program will assist me in this ongoing search.

Insanity and Sanity

Step Two offers the solution to my powerlessness and is a most comforting step. It addresses my insanity, and I need to acknowledge that if I am to take this step. That is not difficult. I am in touch with my addiction to sugar and grains every day. I also see the effects of others' addictions to those substances all around me at work, where there is an epidemic of morbid obesity. Junk food is everywhere. I have found evidence of that Power Greater than myself in the meetings of GSA. I have seen transformations in my sponsees and people that I meet at GS retreats. I see that this way of life works and keeps us at a moderate weight without obsession. Through the examples of others and through my own experience in staying abstinent in this program, I see that there is a Power Greater than myself who could and did restore me to sanity.

I Came to Believe

What does 'came to believe' mean to me? It means that I am willing to try to adjust my belief that there is no Higher Power to a more optimistic view that there is a possibility of a higher consciousness. I am hopeful that if I expand my perspective, I may be able to develop my sense of a Higher Power instead of keeping that which was taught to me. By being hopeful I am becoming more autonomous.

'Came to believe' means I totally understand and trust that 'God could and would if sought.' God will restore me to sanity if I align myself with God. The insanity, craziness, or madness I experienced were part of my insane behaviors concerning out-of-control eating. Trying to control these made them worse. Sanity today means I am of sound mind and can live my life - I can solve problems. When I weigh and measure, good things happen in my life, and I am present to experience true living. I can spend my day connected to my life instead of connected to the food. This program guides my day and my life. The 'came, came to and then came to believe' path - I accept that more than ever because I have a Higher Power in my life. That Power can restore me to sanity as I continue in my recovery.

Acceptance of Step Two

I've accepted Step Two when I am desperate enough to admit my powerlessness over compulsive eating, and I became willing and open-minded enough to see and followed the actions of other recovering GreySheeters. I admit that it is possible for HP to give me the same recovery that has been given to others in GSA. I accept my HP's conditions: it works if I work it.

'Came to believe' only happens for me as my mind clears from the food fog. It is a miracle. Only God can take me out of the food. My Higher Power is the builder of my life, and as I surrender to this, I will gain confidence and trust. Sanity reigns as my food is in its proper place. I have a chance today at a freedom filled life because I'm abstinent.

Unconscious to No Matter What

When I came into recovery, I did not believe in God or a Power greater than myself. When I started in GSA, I was unconscious. 'I came to' meant I came out of the food fog. Then I 'came to believe' in God because I knew I could not put down the food on my own. Only God could remove my obsession to eat. I had tried to do it myself my whole life.

My experience with Step Two is a daily one: I did not believe I could abstain from bingeing. I did not believe that I could follow the food plan. I did not believe that I could be a normal weight. Then I came to believe that I could abstain, follow the GS food plan, and stay at a normal weight for my height, one day at a time. It's not like other programs in which you are abstinent or follow the diet one day and then the next day you cheat. It's a hard, down to earth program with boundaries. The program has power over my disease if I take the actions to follow it No Matter What (NMW.)

Step Two Questions

1. What does "Came, came to, and came to believe" mean to me?
2. What is sanity?
3. In my days before GSA, what did "insanity" mean to me?
4. What do "sanity" and "insanity" mean to me now?
5. What is "a Power greater than myself"?
6. Some say, "I came for the vanity and stayed for the sanity." What does this mean to me?
7. "Clarity of mind" is a phrase that is often used to describe a major benefit of GSA. Do I see this clarity of mind in my life? If so, how do I describe it? What specific examples of clarity of mind are demonstrated in my life?
8. What do I understand as "boundaries" in my life today?
9. How does spirituality play out in my life today?
10. "Accepting what is" is a measure of sanity as compared with "denial." How do the concepts of acceptance and denial apply to me?
11. Do I believe in a Power greater than myself? What is the difference between a belief and idea? What are examples in my life?
12. How am I seeking and accepting a Higher Power?
13. Have I become a victim, a rescuer, or a persecutor? Have I been all three? Give examples. Have I been one more often than another? With new boundaries how can I remove myself from this triangle? How can I create new boundaries? What additional support do I need?
14. How do sanity and persistence relate to each other?
15. Have I come to believe that a Power greater than myself can restore me to sanity? How?
16. Am I willing to share "my experience, strength, and hope" with others as it relates to Step Two? If so, when and how?

Step Three: Made a decision to turn our will and our lives over to the care of God as we understood Him.

After Step Two, having come to believe in a Power greater than ourselves, we are now ready to make a conscious "decision to turn our will and our lives over to the care of God as we understood Him."

Let us examine each part of this statement. "Made a decision" is not a physical action but a mental one, a conscious choice from alternatives. Each person can become willing to choose a spiritual path. Each person has a choice to turn his or her "will and life" over to the care of God. "Will" is defined as mental and emotional choices each person makes daily. "Life" is the physical action of the body, along with one's spirit. The "and" in this step indicates a two-part process. For those who have surrendered their will, yet continued to kill themselves with a knife, fork, and spoon, the work is incomplete. The surrender is also incomplete for those who only accept the physical aspect of compulsive eating. The Third Step offers a complete surrender of both life and will.

However, before any newcomer gives in to despair, a willingness to be willing is sufficient to begin. Additional strength for increased willingness comes after repeated demonstrations of how practical this decision can be. Choosing our food from the GreySheet to turn over to a sponsor or another qualified person is a demonstration of willingness. Weighing and measuring our food one meal at a time without exception is another demonstration. Finally, by eating what we have committed and nothing more or less, we demonstrate surrender.

Some abstaining GreySheeters have reported that the simple act of surrendering each morning, then proceeding through their day, doing what is in front of them in the best way possible that day, produces a sense of calm and peace that sustains them through the worst of life's situations.

They are given the right words for the moment, opportunities that supply what is needed to meet a challenge, and the serenity to accept situations that cannot be changed. This ease comes with nothing more than the simple prayer: "Thy will, not mine, be done" joined with the daily practice of a GreySheet food commitment one day at a time.

Steps One and Two precede Step Three for a reason. The steps are taken to allow the admission of defeat and unmanageability based on human resources, followed by coming to believe that a Power greater than oneself can and will restore us to sanity. This understanding for some people comes after belief in something that holds us in regard or love. For some of us we need to change our HP to a Higher Power that we always wanted. This is a higher power that is kind, loving, and interested in us. This is not the "Vengeful Old Guy," which one member envisioned as her Higher Power: a tall figure, wearing a stovepipe hat and wielding a mallet, ready to exterminate vermin such as herself. Her sponsor wisely urged her to discard that power and adopt a more loving one before attempting Step Three. Having come to believe in a Higher Power that cares about our well-being, only then do we arrive at the decision of Step Three. At Step Three we acknowledge our need to experience that care.

We realize at this point that our lives had been misaligned - half of us had been concerned only with ourselves. We had been selfish, self-obsessed, ego-maniacal. The other half - the opposite, dying due to concern for others, wanting the world to like us, and then letting everyone walk all over us. In both of these extremes, the food was the Evil Big Boss dictating our lives.

All of us had the same blockage of our Spiritual arteries: grudges, fears, shame, and guilt, real and imagined. We couldn't be the people we were meant to be because we couldn't accept the world as it *is*, or work in the position we were given, children of God. We are no better or worse than anyone else, but we do have clear marching orders: "Go forth and make this place a better one than it was on the day you were born!"

Many prayers have been used by members to turn their will and lives over to the care of God. Here's an example: "God, I bring to thee my whole self: mind, body, emotions, and spirit to use as You will. Release me from self-centered fear, that I might better do Thy will. Allow me to become what You would have me be. Remove from me the limitations that keep me from accepting Your will. Free me from obstacles that hinder the demonstration of Your light, love, and power to those You would have me help. With each moment of inspiration, make me a container of Your love and Your light. Thy will, not mine, be done."

Whenever we fall short, we can restore our willingness with a prayer. The hope in this act quickly stokes the flame of the decision and reaffirms Step Three. Whether one uses this prayer or chooses another, willingness is the key. Only a small amount is needed to begin a relationship with Higher Power and to continue working the program.

God is unchanging; however, "God, as we understood God," is ever changing, as our ethics, morals, values, and awareness expand and change. Our path gets better defined as we strive daily to learn how to align our will with God's will. As we gain more experience with the program, often the path becomes easier to follow.

It is our decision whether or not to choose an attitude of gratitude for the experiences we receive. A common observation of new GreySheeters is an evolving attitude. Imagine a traveler arriving at a point where one must choose between two doors: one door decorated with the Greek mask of tragedy and the other with the comedy mask. The individual will choose the attitude with which to continue the journey and will pass through the selected door, unaware that there is only one path on the other side.

One abstinent GSA member described her Third Step experience this way: "By turning over my will and life to God, as I understand Him, I choose optimism, hope, and faith that 'This too shall pass...' and the belief that my Higher Power's will for my life will manifest inwardly and outwardly in body, mind, and spirit. I am not a victim. I choose life, abundance, health, a positive attitude, and gratitude. Then I ask, 'What is the next right action?' As long as I do the footwork and leave the results up to my God, the future unfolds one moment at a time in this eternal now. I need not fear because God is always with me."

Another member affirms: "I really believe that there is a Power greater than myself that dwells within me and around me and loves me and cares for me and wants nothing for me but my well-being and growth." Step Three is a decision point, whether the words of these members appeal to you or you develop your own.

For some, the beliefs of fellow GSAs are difficult to comprehend. Remember, the only requirement is to search for a relationship that works for you. Some have found the group as a whole has capabilities that individuals do not. For them, the group can serve as their Higher Power. Many GSA members have come to utilize other spiritual beliefs as they continue to practice this Step. Finding 'something' to which one can surrender is essential.

Many find that making the decision to turn our wills and lives over to the care of God, as we understood God, is necessary to take the remaining steps of GSA. Other steps lie before us. Let us remember, willingness is crucial and only a tiny amount is required to begin.

"God, grant me the Serenity to accept the things I cannot change,

Courage to change the things I can, and the Wisdom to know the difference."

"Thy will not mine be done."

(There is a longer version of the Serenity Prayer for those who wish to use it.)

Personal Step Three Experiences:

"Either God is Everything or Nothing."

"Either God is everything or nothing." The decision is mine. Prior to taking the Third Step, I must become willing to give everything to God. Then I pray for God to allow me to release one item. (Some items on my list include career, sex, children, household, auto, finances, relationships, and perceptions of others.) I then examine my willingness to release previous items I've reviewed. I repeat these actions until I've given the entire list to God. Then I ask God to relieve me of the bondage of self and rest assured that I have stepped away from everything that stands between me and God."

Multiple Paths to God for There is Nowhere Else to Go

* "Willpower used rightly aligns my will with God's will for me."
* "The Third Step is a daily reprieve from compulsive eating."
* "Each day I turn my life and will over to God's care. The more dependent I am on God, the more independent I can be in other matters. I no longer fear loneliness, depression, time constraints, anything or anyone. God is in charge of everything, including my calendar. Therefore I can live gracefully one day at a time. Anytime I once again attempt to manage my life, I instantly re-affirm my willingness by turning my life and will over to God."

* "Some people I know take Step Three inventories by describing a situation in three sentences and then asking themselves the following: "What did I do wrong?" and "What would God expect me to do instead?""
* I am aware how crucial Step Three is. It's not easy. I still have a problem recognizing what's God's will and what is mine.
* Step Three is encouraging me to be open to HP's will, to pray and accept the life as it is and the things that come. I am not the one who is running the show. God is.
* I am surrendered to my Higher Power. I continue to turn over my life and will to the care of my Higher Power daily. In the particularly difficult moments, I may turn over my will again. I do the footwork of service with and for others in order to be in alignment with my HP's will for me. One day at a time I strive to do what is in front of me to be done. I cannot accomplish more than I can do willingly! When I am at odds with everything and everybody, I do not seem to be in alignment with God's will for me. Sometimes, I do need to do what is in front of me, even when there are others that oppose it. Perhaps their HP's will for them is that opposition or perhaps I am misinterpreting something. I pray. I can follow my path and continue to do what is in front of me to do. The outcomes are in HP's "hands."
* I can make choices. I can grow. I can be of service. I can choose to connect with others and give service to GreySheeters Anonymous and to those who are willing to *do* the program. I continue to ask for guidance and willingness. I do this one day at a time. I desire to be in alignment with Higher Power's will for me. I desire to do Higher Power's will for me. 'Thy will not mine be done.' I can be in the space of open possibility as I surrender to my Higher Power.

Step Three Questions:

1. What was my belief regarding a Higher Power before GSA? What is it now?
2. What was "my life" before GSA, and what is it today?
3. What was "my will" before GSA, and what is it today?
4. Have I made a decision to turn over my life and my will? If I have not yet surrendered, what blocks me from making such a decision?

5. What actions can I take daily to renew and deepen my contact with God, as I understand Him?
6. What differences are there on the days when I take this step, compared with the days when I neglect it?
7. Why do some say, "Willingness is the key?"
8. How have I expressed my willingness? What have been the results? What keeps me from surrendering more willingly?
9. How many times in a day do I turn over my will and life? Why is this necessary?
10. What is "the care of God?"
11. How can I increase my willingness to surrender each day?
12. How is my willingness to be of service connected to God's will for me and the power to carry it out?
13. In what ways can I know what God's will is for me today? What is footwork or my effort to accomplish what is in front of me to be done, compared with 'my will'? What is my relationship to the results?
14. How can I be more open and accepting today?
15. How do I know that I have turned over my life and will to God today?

Step Four: Made a searching and fearless moral inventory of ourselves.

We are now at Step Four. This is the turning point. Some who have feared the inventory too much have returned to eating and other behaviors that no longer served them. Why? It might be due to fear of facing what has been and is looking at us, today. What have we to fear, in reality? We have already lived through whatever it was we lived through. We did not die. We lived to tell the tales. Will we die because of what we reveal now? Unlikely. Some of us were threatened with death; however, there are ways in which to dodge threats meant to invoke fear: first is to talk with a sponsor, spiritual adviser, or trusted person to determine the best manner in which to proceed. We know that completion of the preceding three steps is essential to prepare for Step Four.

This step requires us to take a searching and fearless moral inventory of ourselves. This is a written inventory and includes all our past and present liabilities and assets, as we understand them now. Future steps will deal with future issues. For now, we focus on the elements of our character and personalities that have brought us to this moment.

Looking to the past, we realize that many of the character issues that have combined with our compulsive eating have created confusion. We did not find ourselves in GSA by accident. The circumstances of our lives have brought us to this program. We have come with a set of beliefs about how others and ourselves, "should" be.

We have carried grudges and resentments that have crippled us. We have fears that have kept us from releasing old ideas that imprisoned us in eating prior to GSA. Some of us have the baggage of sexual dysfunction and beliefs that have hindered our progress emotionally toward healthy personal growth and emotional development. Our relationships, based on our early dysfunctional ideas, went with us into the work world, communities, intimate relationships, and our self-evaluations.

Some of our beliefs, self-centered in the extreme, have clouded our understanding of what is the reality of others in our lives. We are asleep, dreaming we are awake. Only with a fearless moral inventory can we begin to clear away the wreckage of the past and present, arising from our deep delusional slumber to see the patterns that have kept us enslaved to our old ideas for so long!

Will Step Four free us from all of the difficulties our old ideas, behaviors, and beliefs produced? It depends on how thoroughly we are willing to take this step and all the steps that precede and follow it. The Steps of GSA are a solution that only we can limit by our hesitation to take them deeply and completely. The willingness in Step Three applies here, too. When we are willing to complete a thorough Step Four, we will be free to experience the changes promised in subsequent steps. "The change can be a superficial change that is only important for today, or it can be a change that alters the very fabric of my existence." Thus, one longtime member of Twelve Step programs attested to the depth of character change that occurred in her life when she did her first fourth step in GSA.

Now, back to the "should's" and the way life is "supposed" to be, instead of the way it is. For one to thoroughly take this step, a close look at blaming and shaming will open many previously closed doors. The breeze of fresh air that enters through open doors and windows can clear away the gloom and despair caused by previous bouts of irresponsibility and finger pointing. "Freedom from shame about my own being was lifted with this step. I do not have to be ashamed of who I am, for I am one of God's kids!" exclaimed one GSA member. "If I truly believe that God can restore me to sanity, then what becomes possible is a clear-sighted view of what is and of how I can assume responsibility for my life and my choices."

One member emphasized the need to separate any childhood abuse experienced (physical, sexual, and mental/emotional) from the choices and behaviors made following the abuse: "The abuse is never a child's fault! No matter what the child was told, experienced, or came to believe, the child was innocent. God was not responsible for the abuse either. Free will and a sick person's choices were the causes."

To conduct a fearless and thorough moral inventory we need to begin by asking ourselves, "What part did I play, or do I play, in maintaining the old ideas and beliefs that control my behaviors and thoughts?" Let us review personal responsibility in light of the concept of God restoring us to sanity. We turn our wills and lives over to the care of God, as we understand God. With these heartfelt beliefs and actions, all things are possible. According to GSA members' collective experience, strength, and hope, a genuine attempt to carry out Step Four is the beginning.

So, how to begin? Some have found that the task is best done alone, in a defined period, with a Fifth Step previously scheduled with a sponsor. Others have found that Step Four is best taken with a sponsor's guidance, but without thought or concern for what comes next. We write an inventory for ourselves and for the freedom and clarity that come from doing this form of spiritual, mental, and emotional housecleaning.

GreySheeters often comment on how the household and mental clutter seems to evaporate with the clarity that comes with GSA abstinence. This may be the physiological clearing away of the sensitivities to grains and sugars and the clearing of the fog that had accompanied those substances in our minds and bodies. The behaviors produced by those substances and the choices made with the chemically altered minds shift with the inventory, and the beginning of a new path appears.

The Fourth and Fifth Steps go together. This is why some members choose after they have written their Fourth Step to answer the Fifth Step Questions before starting to share the inventory. When participating in an AWOL on the phone, some choose to answer the Fifth Step questions prior to sharing the Fourth Step answers.

Those who have done many turns of Twelve Step work and specifically Step Four writing may be surprised at the outcomes of this application of Step Four. The benefits of the clarity of mind that GSA abstinence produces can be surprising. During previous years of recovery in other Twelve Step programs, grain and sugar consumption clouded minds and imposed limitations on members' vision. GSA abstinence grants clarity of mind to perform a truly thorough and fearless moral inventory.

Whatever method chosen to address the past debris and its effect on the present, the future can be as 'sparkly new' and 'squeaky clean' as we choose to have it be. Willingness is still the key. The insights and self-awareness grown from our fearless and thorough moral inventories are nothing short of miraculous. Come join us on this road. Fear need not be a part of this trip because our past choices are no longer relevant. Now our lives and wills are turned over to God, as we understand God. The present is a gift from God, given to us each day. That is why it is called the *present*. Join us in opening all our gifts this day.

In the Fourth Step, we are going to look at our assets and our liabilities. Let us begin with writing down all our assets we can think of now and then continue adding to the list. Acknowledging our assets may be more demanding than listing our liabilities. This might be true for some compulsive eaters, as their demand for perfection has often caused them to belittle their imperfect but considerable assets.

What character assets do we now have? What character assets do we aspire to express? Let us consider our positives. Are we loving, kind, compassionate, generous, grateful, forthright, empathetic, creative, genuine, honest, hopeful, spiritual, accepting of self and others, accepting of what IS, faithful, charitable, steadfast, mature, contented, peaceful, respectful, optimistic, and free from judgments of self and others? Do we aspire to be lifelong learners? Do we conduct our lives with integrity?

Additionally, a willingness to continue to examine the unexamined portions of life and self; the release of regrets, resentments and fears; and restraint of tongue, pen, email, and thought might be additional positives. Lists of character assets can include many more items. A wise sponsor invites, "Please add your assets to your list. Assess yourself positively. Aspire to what you believe God would have you be, do, have, and become. What would you become if you were free from your personal restraints? What might your life be without these limitations? What could your life mean to the world?"

There are many different ways to do the Fourth Step. Here are several methods GSA members have followed. Different ways may be appropriate at different times in abstinence. A friend of ours in an older Twelve Step program suggested the following brief inventory be answered as completely and thoroughly as possible:

"1. In looking back over your life, what memories are still painful, are ones that you still feel guilty about, and still make you feel '*dirty*'?
2. Today, what do you conceive as your *defects of character*?
3. Who do you resent...and why? (Be as specific and as nasty as you feel!)
4. In what ways do you feel inadequate as a person?

5. What are the natures of the on-going problems you have in personal relationships, such as with your family or other people close to you?
6. What are your goals in life as you see them today, whether they seem "realistic" or not?
7. Do you see any way that the program can help you begin to make progress toward any of these goals?"

(This friend was thanked by the co-founder of a previous Twelve Step program for his assistance when that program for food related issues was newly founded.)

Another friend suggests that three questions form the basis of an inventory:

1. What makes me angry?
2. What makes me happy?
3. What do I want to be when I grow up?

If we practice this daily inventory system, what might we expect the results to be? Might we be surprised?

Another friend divides life into seven year overlapping increments, e.g., 0-7, 7-14, 14-21, 21-28, etc. Writing about each increment of time and the associated people, places, and experiences helps clarify material for an autobiographical inventory. This sometimes aids those who are reluctant to do any other inventory. Insights are gained as increments fill or remain blank at times.

What other areas might be fruitful for inventory? For centuries now, *the seven deadly sins* have been a means of inventory taking. One woman suggested that they might be called *the plagues*, because they have harmed most of us and wreaked havoc on civilizations over time. The word plagues reminds us of the anagram PLAGGES: Pride, Lust, Anger, Greed, Gluttony,

Envy, and Sloth. Pride is first on the list. Many of us would agree that most of our troubles come from pride or a lack of humility: either wanting to be better than others or failing to be the best. Lust has carried some of us into humiliating and harmful circumstances that have hurt us, as well as, our children, spouses, family members, and friends. For others, health and business have been ruined by lust. Our anger has set off rages that were the outcomes of food-driven ravages. Stymied by greed for prestige in the form of accomplishments, recognition, money, and political office, some took what was not theirs. We used and then abused others to get MORE. Gluttony was central to our issues. There was never enough food to quiet the unending hunger that drove us. Overindulgence and excessive consumption are hallmarks of gluttony.

We have a disease that has physiological, mental, emotional, and spiritual parts. The phenomenon of craving is the marker of the disease. A desire for food to do something *for or to* us may not be gluttony. In fact, many of us have wanted food to soothe us and to fill us in ways that have not been in accord with our physical needs. The cravings were never satisfied for long. The behaviors we used to minimize the cravings, in the end, only exaggerated them into a caricature of well-being that was grounded in self-loathing and disgust. Most of us have the disease *and* gluttony.

In an Icelandic documentary on GreySheeters Anonymous, the English translation for compulsive overeater was 'uncontrollable glutton'; however, food addiction is central to what our GSA program addresses.

To continue *the plagges*, envy in our bellies increased our physical hunger for food or fed our self-hatred, envy's hallmark characteristic. Some said, "I am not enough, or I am not good enough; I need more, and I must have what you have to fill me up." There is not enough access to money, possessions (real or imagined), relationships, or other human resources to fill our empty souls. Lastly, sloth kept us from making the commitments to others and ourselves to change. We were lazy. Our cars, bedrooms, and desks were evidence of our physical sloth. We were unwilling and unable to ask a Higher Power for help to surrender. We stayed stuck. The Seven Deadly Sins offer productive inventory options. Pride, lust, anger, greed, gluttony, envy, and sloth are available to review in their milder forms as well.

In another way to address a Fourth Step, we list all those persons, animals, institutions, beliefs, and organizations that we resent or feel anger toward. Sometimes God is on our list. For most, some resentments towards ourselves are on the list. As one member describes it, "I resented myself for the things I did to myself and others while under the influence of grains and sugars. Sometimes I said and did even worse things when I was coming off of the carbs: withdrawal rage and depression." Other resentments harbored against ourselves were for the child unborn, an apology not made before a person died, or the 'unforgivable' expectations we placed on others or ourselves. What was hidden beneath these? Often it was fear we would lose something we treasured or fear of failing to gain something we wanted.

Now let us look at our resentment list, item by item, and complete a chart. Some members use a spiral notebook with the pages folded in half to create columns. In the first resentment column write the person, animal, institution, belief, or organization's name. In the second column, the answer to the question, "What is the resentment?" Be specific. The specificity helps clear up not only this particular item but also how it fits with all the other items on this list, on the other lists, and in the other inventory items. Be brief; brevity clarifies. In the third column, note the impact. For instance, is the impact on personal relations with others, sex relations, self-esteem, finances, or a relationship with God? Perhaps this resentment affects more than one aspect of our personality. In the fourth column, the most significant question is answered: "What is my part?" Some have found that *"my part"* was staying in abusive situations as adults or keeping a child in harm's way, or some other specific choices of thoughts and behavior.

Specificity and clarity in this column support further step work. Some inventory-takers include a fifth column for each resentment. Five sentences: 1. Where was I self-seeking? 2. Where was I dishonest? 3. Where was I fearful? 4. How did I play a part before? 5. How did I play a part after?

Again, be mindful that in childhood, the child is not responsible for anything. In childhood abuse, there is nothing that the child could change. The opportunity to change comes when the child matures to adulthood. As an adult, the adult choices may be based on old ideas originating with the childhood abuse. These adult choices are the responsibility of the adult. As adults, we can individually ask, "What can I do differently now? In what ways can I change my actions now? What are the actions that have, in fact, come as a result of my old behaviors and ideas?"

Next, let us list our fears. Simply listing "I am afraid of...." *over and over again* until each and every fear has been put down on paper helps to identify this arena for further discovery.

After we complete our fears list, there are many ways that have been suggested to deal with each fear. The simplest way is first to classify each fear as *life-threatening* versus *not life threatening.* Allow reality to be your guide. Some fears protect us from harm and are *hard-wired* into our beings. Do we need to be afraid of leaping from high places? Probably, under most circumstances this fear can be useful to our survival. Do we currently need to be afraid of falling from commercial aircraft? Probably not. So what fears are ones that we need to look at carefully and ask Higher Power to remove?

If I fear that I am not enough, or I fear the judgment of others, what have I done to myself? If I fear the unknown and experience a sense of panic, independent of the external reality, what have I done to myself? In what ways might I have limited myself from what God would have me be, do, become, and have? In what ways does the word 'should' enter into my fears? "I should be unafraid; I should be above all of this; I should…." Each of us can fill in the character defects that limit us in our thoughts and deeds.

Each of us has the same number of seconds, minutes, and hours in a day as every other person. How we individually choose to use those moments determines what happens next and to some degree even the number of days in our lives. "To the degree that I limit myself with my fears, to that degree I limit what I can become, as well as what I am today. To the degree that I limited my past health with unhealthy choices, I limit the future; to the degree that I choose healthfully today, I expand future possibilities," observed one GSA member. He continued, "How have my fears manifested as limitations in my life? What might letting go of particular fears allow? Am I willing to more completely take Step Three with these thoughts in mind? If so, what then? If not, why not?"

Another area to inventory is sex. This includes both thoughts and behaviors. The questions about sex need to be specific. In what ways and in what circumstances were my choices based on selfishness, self-centeredness, and old beliefs that I had to have more? My food addictions were infrequently the only addictions. Sex and sexual acting-out have been behaviors that many of us can now acknowledge and inventory. On the other hand, some of us have been anorexic in this area and needed to address that. We look for alternatives and guidance, including asking for release from excesses and restrictions. For example, when we prepare ourselves for the day at work or an event, we consider appropriate clothing, attitude, and behavior that suit our newly found body, personality, and commitment. Just as we try on clothes and sometimes take them off because we decide that they don't fit that day or moment, we can also try on new behaviors and new attitudes. Just as we choose to share positive pitches at GSA meetings, we can choose positive actions in our daily lives, and we can strive to do this with the same integrity with which we now commit, weigh, and measure our food. With GSA abstinence, we gain clarity in our choices about deeds and attitudes, as well as food.

Some additional questions that GreySheeters may ask in Step Four are: "In what ways have I harmed myself and others with my appetites for food, sex, society, and security? In what ways have I tried to get back at others for deeds that were not their responsibility? In what ways have I taken out my anger, resentment, fears, and sexual appetites on others to harm them and myself? In what ways have I harmed myself? In what ways have I expressed my anger at God and my fear of God?"

Some other possible questions to answer in an inventory are the following: "Is there anything about myself that I find objectionable? Is there anything that I find objectionable about others? Do any of these overlap?" Many of us have found that the items that we find most objectionable in the personalities or behaviors of others we recognize in ourselves. We found that we either deny something that is within us or we project it outwards on others. Often when we tried to eradicate a behavior that made us unhappy, we wanted everyone to eradicate the same behavior for now and all eternity. Take for example the ex-cigarette smoker who can no longer tolerate smokers in the environment. Are we similar?

Dishonesty and denial kept our prison doors locked. The willingness to ask for help (or even just the willingness to ask for the willingness to be willing) was not ours at the time. Hidden in the self-imposed darkness of dishonesty and denial is our self-deceit; the ruin of *the plagges* continued. Only when we admitted complete defeat, did the *beginning of the end* of this imprisonment appear. In our Fourth Step inventory we often ask, "In what ways am I still dishonest and deceitful with myself, if not with others?" Realizing this is an ongoing process. We can think for example: "Yes, murder is wrong, but I have never murdered anyone. (Not with a weapon other than my thoughts, tongue, and eyes.)" Or "I rarely harmed another with my deeds." However, stepping free of deceit, we might see more clearly that the absence of actions, the absence of honesty to enhance a relationship, or the absence of our love, support, or empathy harmed another. Had we instead chosen to be available to serve, to give to another, to break another's chains with our own honest self-acceptance and heartfelt sharing, would we have helped make the world a better place?"

"Had I been less self-involved, how might I have used my talents and gifts to lighten the burden of another? Would the world be better if I had acted on my ideas, had written the letter I never wrote, birthed the children I never had, loved the children that others had if it was too late for birthing, or completed the work I had previously left unfinished?" These questions might indicate the direction for additional inventory work.

What if and *if only* instances have been their plagges. "How might I identify the severe limitations I have put on my willingness to do God's will in the world? How have I kept myself from being used in positive ways that might have made a difference for others? Am I willing now to let go of the grandiosity that has in the past kept me not only too big, but also too small? Perhaps I am and have always been, up to the task. Is now the time to grow into my capabilities? I need no longer play God. I can be the person I am meant to be and allow that to be enough.

For the Fourth Step inventory, we asked, "In what circumstances have I overshot the mark, exaggerated my talents or diminished them? When have I accomplished too little or too much? Have I demanded too much? If so, when? Were food, attention, college degrees, money, property, prestige, and some other tangible or emotional commodity too important or too unimportant to me? Where is the balance? What is enough? How might I find the balance point in my life today? What strategies might I use to weigh and measure life as I do my food? How might I make and hold commitments with integrity in other areas, as I do with the food on the scale? How might I offer the same kindness and grace within boundaries to others and myself, as my sponsor does concerning my mistakes?

Am I as harsh and unforgiving with others, as I perceive others to have been with me? How might I learn compassion and replace my inquisition-like demands on myself and others? Is there a place for perfection in GSA?

Do I need to use a jeweler's scale with 3 digits to the right of the decimal point on myself and others or might a scale with one or two digits or a cup and a measuring spoon leveled and wiped be sufficient for food? What is the balance point, and what is enough for us today?"

"What standards do we set for ourselves and others? What standard do we demand of ourselves and others? Are we willing to accept the loving compassion of our sponsor or another qualified person who says, 'Let it go'? If not, why not? What keeps us requiring more or less, in the same way as our cravings demanded more or less food?"

We asked ourselves, "How might we look to a Higher Power to reveal the *perfection* that God would have us experience today?" If we are new to the program, do we demand that all of the weight be vaporized immediately, or do we accept that time is necessary to change? Change comes for most of us in gradual increments. To demand that the future be right now is not only unrealistic and selfish, but it is impossible, too. We have found that life is a process. Starting now, we can be willing to change. In the future, we can be willing to change more.

Forgiveness for ourselves and others may allow more changes to occur than all the battering of self and others had ever accomplished. A loving concern for self and others may permit hoped for changes to unfold, even when unexpected. In terms of inventory, in what circumstances have we been unforgiving? When, and under what circumstances have we been critical of ourselves and others? How have we expressed this critical nature, and under what circumstances might this be adjusted or corrected entirely?

Last, but not least, if we are still blaming another for anything done to us, when can we let it go? Holding on to ancient hurts binds us to the pain of the past. What benefit is gained from old ideas that don't work? Why not live in the present? As one newcomer expressed so poignantly, "It is hard to live each moment in the present holding myself responsible for my choices and actions. I can't manage the past, too!" Such truth!

After writing the Fourth Step inventory, let us look for just a moment at the outcome. Is there anything left unwritten? Are there any hidden secrets? For one's own *best* good, let it all be written. Let it all be put on paper. Let God and the future determine with whom to share the details we might still wish to leave unspoken.

"If we let go of the past with all the limitations we have created for ourselves, what now might be different? How might we talk to ourselves differently? How might we communicate with others? What changes might we experience in preferences in food, clothing, behavior, emotional needs, thoughts, and words? Would we keep all of the commitments, clutter, belongings, old clothing, control issues, hatreds, fears, societal beliefs, negatives, and blaming attitudes we once held? What creativity, productivity, mindfulness, and spirituality might manifest instead? What if the one choice were to let go of procrastination or sloth? How might peace, humor, well-being, harmony, authenticity, and serenity be new characteristics of the inner voice? How might enjoyment and delight manifest in this new life daily, instead of the pressure of never-ending comparisons, judgments, and demands? How might the Light, Wholeness, and Love of God shine through each person?

For our own good, we write it all down on paper. By doing this, freedom comes.

Ongoing growth allows us to see what we believe now to be negative can in the future be used for God's purposes as we share our experience, strength, and hope with another.

Forgiveness for ourselves and others allows more changes to occur than all the anger ever accomplished. Concern and empathy for ourselves and others may permit changes to unfold. Lead being turned into gold never happened for the alchemists, but in GSA we who were negative and useless are transformed by the steps into gold to be shared with others to ease their burdens.

Dishonesty and denial kept the prison doors locked. The willingness to ask for help, the willingness to ask for the willingness to be willing, was not ours at the time. Hidden in the self-imposed darkness of the dishonesty and denial of our self-deceit, the ruin of "the plagges" continued. Only when we admitted complete defeat, did the beginning of the end of this imprisonment come. The steps taken in order make this possible.

Personal Fourth Step Experiences:

Food, Love, Money

The Fourth Step makes it evident that I find it very difficult to find assets within myself. The Fourth Step helps me see that my selfishness arises because I feel that I do not have enough of myself to give away. Doing another Fourth Step has helped me see the beginnings of my defects. I thought that the abuse and neglect that I suffered formed me. It has taken an enormous amount of time and energy to work on myself. Many of the defects that I have named in previous Fourth Steps are the same that I named this time, but the pain has diminished. One of the biggest revelations doing this step is the insane amount of money that I spend on prepared foods.

My spending is harming my ability to save for future financial stability. I've realized that I am doing with the money what I did with food: spending what I want without caring about the consequences. I know that I will not have enough money to live on after I retire if I fail to save. I know that I have been destroying my future and have been unwilling to do anything to curtail myself. I am still a slave to food in this context. I am afraid of feeling pain when I say "No" to myself regarding food I want. My finances and food are intermingled. Giving up compulsive eating and bingeing when I first got into the program was the hardest thing that I had EVER done, except admitting that my mother did not love me. I think I am waiting to be struck monetarily abstinent. That didn't work with food, and it isn't working with money.

Change Process

Step Four is teaching me to look honestly at my mistakes, my wrongdoings and my unsuitable behaviors toward others. By writing things down and then sharing my inventory, I open the possibility to be more aware when I again do these things or to adjust before I do them. I also can see what needs to be done. I have done the Fourth and the Fifth steps before, and I plan to continue them. I know this is an ongoing thing as I'm sometimes aware of some things I'm doing wrong and then the next time something else comes to the surface. To stay abstinent I have been taught to do the Steps; so I'm taking the actions, learning, and trying to change or accept. This is ongoing work.

In the next pages, GreySheeters will find numbered questions indicating potential directions for further inventory work. A step sponsor and sponsee might review the questions to identify those to be addressed in this particular inventory. A selection (random or specific) may be useful. Some choose to answer all of the questions each time. (These are questions from the reading above.)

Step Four Questions:

1. Is there anything about myself that I find objectionable?
2. Is there anything that I find objectionable about others?
3. Do any of these overlap?
4. In what ways have I harmed myself and others with my appetites for food, sex, society, and security?
5. In what ways have I sought payback from others for deeds for which they were not responsible?
6. In what ways have I taken out on others my anger, resentment, fears, and sexual appetites to harm them and me?
7. In what ways have I harmed myself?
8. In what ways have I expressed my fears to God and my anger at God?
9. In what circumstances have I overshot the mark: exaggerating my talents or diminishing them? Accomplishing too little or too much?
10. Have I been demanding excess? If so, in what instances? Was it food, attention, college degrees, money, property, prestige, or some other emotional or tangible commodity?
11. Where is the balance? How might I find the balance point in my life today?
12. What is "enough" for me today?
13. What strategies might I use to weigh and measure life similar to the process I use with my food?
14. How might I make and hold commitments with integrity in areas outside of the food on the scale as with the food on the scale?
15. How might I offer the same kindness and grace within boundaries to others and myself as my sponsor does concerning my mistakes?
16. Am I as harsh and unforgiving with others as I perceive others to have been with me? How might I learn compassion in place of inquisition-like demands on others and myself?
17. What is the place of perfection in GreySheeters Anonymous? Do I try to achieve more and more perfection by using scales with 3 or more digits after the decimal point or by eliminating food item after food item to feel more "perfect"?
18. What standard do I set for myself and others?
19. What standard do I demand of myself and others?

20. Am I willing to accept the loving compassion of my sponsor or another qualified person who says, 'Let it go'? If not, why not?
21. What keeps me requiring more or less, in the same way as my cravings demanded more or less food?
22. How might I look to a Higher Power to reveal the "perfection" that I believe God would have me experience today?
23. If I am relatively new to the program, do I demand that all of the weight or exterior manifestations of my disease be eliminated immediately, or do I accept that time is necessary to have time?
24. In what circumstances have I been unforgiving?
25. When and under what circumstances have I been critical of myself and others? How have I expressed this critical nature?
26. In what circumstances might my critical nature be adjusted or redressed entirely?
27. In what ways am I still dishonest and deceitful with myself, if not with others?
28. If I am available to serve, to give to another, to break another's chains with my honest self-acceptance and heartfelt sharing, might the world be a better place? What might I choose?
29. If I am less self-involved, might I better use the talents and gifts I have to lighten the load of another?
30. Might the world be different had I acted on ideas I never acted on, or written the writing I never did, or birthed the children I never had, or completed the work I left unfinished? How might I release these hypothetical burdens?
31. How might I identify the severe limitations I have put on my willingness to do HP's will in the world?
32. How have I kept myself from being used, not only in negative but positive ways that could now make a difference for others if I were to change?
33. Am I willing now to let go of the *lack of humility* that has in the past kept me not only too big but also too small?
34. Perhaps am I and have I always been up to the task for many more tasks than I had thought myself capable?
35. Is now the time to grow into my capabilities?
36. Do I need to stop playing God? Can I be the person I am meant to be and allow that to be enough?

37. If I am still blaming another or holding another to account for anything done to me, what might I let go? Is the holding on binding me to the pain and the past?
38. What benefit do I gain from holding on to an old idea of what I was or was not or could have been or could not have been?
39. Why not live in the present?
40. If I let go of the past with all the limitations it has created for my SELF, what now might be different?
41. How might I talk to myself differently?
42. How might I communicate with others?
43. What changes might I experience in preferences in food, clothing, behavior, thoughts, words, and emotional or tangible needs?
44. Would I keep all of the commitments, clutter, belongings, old clothing, control issues, hatreds, fears, societal beliefs, negatives, and blaming attitudes I once held? What am I willing to let go?
45. What creativity, productivity, mindfulness, and spirituality might manifest instead?
46. What if the one choice were to let go of procrastination and sloth?
47. How might enjoyment and delight manifest in this new life daily?
48. Instead of the pressure of never-ending comparisons, judgments, and demands, how might peace, humor, well-being, harmony, authenticity, and serenity be new characteristics of the inner voice?
49. Does my enhanced ability to see assets in myself expand my ability to see assets in others?
50. Have I left anything unwritten?
51. Are there any secrets still hidden from myself or the other to whom this may be read?

Step Five: Admitted to God, to ourselves, and to another human being the exact nature of our wrongs.

In Step Four, we wrote a searching and fearless moral inventory. Now, we ask ourselves if there is anything that we have omitted. Is fear of sharing our secrets with another person keeping us from completing the inventory process? If the answer is yes, then we have not finished the inventory. We do not need to keep our worst liabilities hidden because of the fear of sharing them. Many of us have experienced this discomfort and then discovered it disappeared in doing this step.

Are there additional assets that we were unable to recognize and list in the Fourth Step? After finishing the inventory, we can move forward, knowing we have gained insights into our behavior, thoughts, and feelings. We are now ready to share the truth about ourselves with God and another human being aloud.

It is important to consider carefully with whom to share the inventory. It needs to be someone who understands that it is a sacred responsibility to hold the confidences described in the inventory. A spouse or someone involved in the inventory is not eligible due to the nature of the material and the relationship. Most GSA members choose to share inventory with a trusted sponsor or another participant in a GSA step study group. Some of us choose to share a part of the inventory with a spiritual or religious confidante, a psychologist, or a therapist. The most important thing is to complete the Fifth Step.

A face-to-face meeting in a quiet, private place with sufficient time is the ideal situation. It is certainly preferable to be physically present; however, in our worldwide fellowship, some of us will share the inventory over the phone or through online services.

Upon beginning the Fifth Step, we ask God to be with us to hear the inventory and to guide our thoughts and words. Some of us share a moment of silence to acknowledge the presence of a Higher Power. Others place a chair in the line of sight of the 5th stepper. This too is recognition of Higher Power's presence. Whatever we choose, we recognize that we are "admitting to God, to ourselves, and to another human being the exact nature of our wrongs."

The choices we make fall into the category of 'my part in it.' The solitary and important exception to responsibility for 'my part in it' is the experience of child abuse. Sometimes, even as adults, we carry the false message that as children we caused the inappropriate and harmful actions of adults or older young people. Children are not responsible for those actions. What we have done as a result of our childhood abuse or other harming experiences is our responsibility to address.

In Step Five we share all the dark secrets and hidden motivations of our character. In each instance, we look carefully at our role in the circumstance that caused us pain, remorse, shame, guilt, or any other intense emotion. Only by seeing the part that we played in the drama of our lives do we begin to see the potential for change allowed by acceptance of responsibility for our past actions.

It has been said that the actions of others may act as a mirror for our behavior. The sharing of our inventory with God and another human being permits and invites the opening up of ourselves to recognize that while we were injured, we in turn injured others. We know that 'hurt people hurt people.' We cannot undo the harm that has already been done, but by wholeheartedly taking this step, we accept ourselves and experience a previously unknown peace.

As individuals, we have experienced the pitfalls of the human condition. We all believed we were unique. Sometimes that uniqueness isolated us, but with the sharing of our inventories, we learn we are part of the human race. During the Fifth Step, the recipient of the inventory will likely share some similar experiences. We will recognize that we have things in common with other GreySheeters - the retelling of our stories, through Fifth Stepping, helps us to eradicate the sense that 'I am so different as to be unlovable.' Each of us is lovable and capable of moving on to what we are meant to do and be in the world.

Before ending our inventory, we take the time to ask ourselves once more if there is any other information that we need to share. When we disclose the secrets we thought could never see the light of day, we find they lose their power.

Step Five is not just for ourselves. Each of our Step Five experiences is turned into treasure available to share with another compulsive eater or food addict. When the people with whom we share our inventory share with us, each of us releases the habit of isolation. Through this process, we allow our Higher Power to change us, so we can increasingly be of more service to God and others. We share our assets and liabilities and move forward through the remaining steps. We are on the path of freedom and responsibility.

Personal Step Five Experiences:

No Longer an Alien

Admitted to God, ourselves, and another human being the exact nature of our wrongs. I freely admit the nature of my wrongs. I am honest and open about my character defects. Doing the fifth step with the AWOL (A Way of Life step study) group lets me see that I am not unique. When others in the group are open and honest about their defects, it helps me to be more honest and not so afraid to reveal my defects. The unwavering honesty others in the group revealed diminishes my feeling of shame that I have had about my shortcomings. It helps me feel less like an alien.

Doing Steps in an AWOL for me means facing my personal history, my character defects, mistakes, and 'wrong deeds.' Then, I share what I have found without trying to perform, apologize, or diminish. The experience of listening to others encourages me. I am sharing the real me without self-criticism or fears of being punished. It is important for my recovery and personal growth to know and accept the whole me with all the bad and good and with all my human limitations.

Doing this Step also fulfills my need to focus on me and talk about me, which was pressed down for so many years under compulsive eating and other sick behaviors. I no longer feel like an alien.

Hand on the Door Knob

I read my long autobiographical inventory to my sponsor, but I had held back one piece of information. I told myself that others knew. I did not have to tell my sponsor. I knew I needed to tell this one person everything. I decided I had nothing to lose as I took my hand from the doorknob. I turned and quietly acknowledged my secret. She was not dismayed or surprised and told me she would see me at the meeting the next evening. She also told me that I had done a thorough inventory. I knew I had done so.

Step Five Questions:

1. How do I determine it is time to do my Fifth Step?
2. With whom am I willing to share the Fourth Step's intimate and personal information about myself?
3. What keeps me from being willing to share my complete inventory with another human being? How can I arrange the sharing?
4. Is it harder to share with another human being than to share with my Higher Power and myself?
5. What keeps me from being willing to do the Fifth Step with my Higher Power, and how can I overcome this?
6. What keeps me from being willing to do the Fifth Step with myself? Is it easy because I delude myself?
7. What positive outcomes do I expect from Step Five?
8. What do I fear about taking a Fifth Step? What can help remove these fears?
9. What allows me to move forward with this Step?
10. What have others experienced as a result of taking the Fifth Step, and what can I learn from their experiences?
11. Am I willing to share my experience of working this Step with other abstinent people? How?

Step Six: Were entirely ready to have God remove all these defects of character.

Now that we have taken a moral inventory and shared it, we prepare a list of character defects, already identified in the Fourth and Fifth Steps.

Are we entirely ready to have God remove all our defects of character? Some of us said, in actions - or lack of them - or words, "No!" Others said, "No we aren't ready, yet." With tenacity, we address this step. "Certainly I am willing to have the most obvious defects of character removed," remarked one member. She continued, "The things that are causing the most difficulties right now can go; however, I still take pleasure in some behaviors and thoughts that others might think are character defects." Others asked, "What would life be without a particular defect or trait? Will we lose ourselves or become a different person?" Fear of the unknown stopped some from letting go.

Character assets may be defects when used to excess. These character traits may have helped us survive in previous parts of our lives and may have served valid purposes then. Are they over-used or overextended now? As an example, detail-oriented and organized may be assets at times, but that can also mean that we are picky and uncompromising.

Character defects may include thoughts without obvious actions or may be actions we think are unimportant. Which one of us has not held lust in mind while pointing a finger at the behaviors of another? Haven't many of us gossiped while pretending to express concern? What about those of us who are not satisfied that we have enough possessions? Those of us who clutter our homes, go into debt, or procrastinate have character defects, too. The defects may be milder and perhaps less deadly than those who rage and seek revenge, but the defects of character are still evident.

Self-seeking, self-centeredness, jealousy, and envy are items found on most members' lists. Others identify being judgmental of themselves and others as a character defect. Being pretentious, arrogant, self-loathing, or unbalanced in some other way might be on the lists of some GSAs. Another person might list a zealous need whether this desire is for power, prestige, material possessions, beauty, a relationship or (only occasionally) character assets.

Thus, the list of our members' character defects may include different degrees of the same items or distinctly different items. Regardless of the list, the key to Step Six is willingness to have our character defects removed.

While sitting alone in meditation or taking a walk in quiet contemplation, we review our experiences with Steps One through Five. Have we completed each step to the best of our ability? Is there anything left undone in the steps that would hinder us from moving forward? Are we ready to engage in a more intimate relationship with our Higher Power? Was the inventory thorough and complete? Did we leave anything out or hold back some item in Step Five? What are the character defects that were evident repeatedly throughout the inventory? What other defects of character materialized as we discussed the inventory? Is there something about which we are still excessively ashamed, guilty, or proud? When a shortcoming continues to serve and has not brought disaster, it is tempting to say, "I will never give this one up," says a newcomer.

A long timer responds, "My sponsor, having learned from experience, always urges me to exchange the word 'not yet' for 'never.'" Such an apparently small adjustment opens the door to allow a sliver of light to pierce the gloom. When we take the risk of letting go of character defects, opportunities for healthy and growth-producing life emerge. Willingness is that powerful.

GreySheeters in conversation say, "What will I be if I give up all of my character defects? If I can't gossip anymore, I will have nothing to say to friends. If I quit being amusingly smart-mouthed and critical, I will end up bland and uninteresting. Lateness may not aid me, but I am a busy person, and I like to add one more job to my day before racing off for an appointment. I know I can multi-task and get everything done. I cannot imagine being on time consistently; I thrive on the thrill of being short on time. If I didn't procrastinate, my life would no longer be on hold, and I might have to act on something that scares me."

Perhaps we love our character defects too much, or maybe they appear to serve us. If I give up my lust, how can I live and breathe? Later, I might find that I do not lust after anyone; I am in love." Our explanations, perhaps are our excuses to hold us in bondage. What other reasons prevent us from letting go of our character defects?

To ignore, avoid, or reject Step Six might seem like an option, but the price is high. If we continue to clutch our character defects, we jeopardize abstinence. Sometimes we long to hold onto the familiar rather than the unknown; however, the freedom that comes from becoming "ready" has gifts beyond measure. "Do I believe that my Higher Power will remove from me the character defects I have seen in my inventory?"

Long timers will respond with a resounding, "Yes! We have seen the results in ourselves and others. Long-standing flaws that caused problems in relationships, stunted self- esteem, and separated us from the Sunlight of the Spirit were removed as a result of becoming entirely ready to have God remove all these defects of character."

This process of using the Twelve Steps in our lives on a daily basis is not only for the believer but also for the faint-hearted and the disbeliever. Everyone can change. Each one only needs the willingness to go forward. Enhanced belief and spirituality are the outcomes of sustained effort. Some have suggested that perfection is neither possible nor desirable.

Long timers have responded, "Perfection is nothing to fear. We have not seen it, yet. This is a lifelong process. We strive each day for progress, not perfection."

What if one of us cries, "No, I will die without this part of my character!" She or he may have chosen a death sentence. Our disease of food addiction can be lethal.

Long timers explain, "Anything that we put between ourselves and abstinence goes." To gain freedom from compulsions and cravings and to gain clarity of mind may not be enough encouragement to take this Step. If not those rewards, then the choice to avoid death, insanity, or unrelenting pain may become the reasons to continue down the path to take Step Six.

We all reach a point where shortchanging ourselves is no longer an option. Our personal limitations no longer hold us back. The moment comes gradually or sometimes between breaths. We reach the point of becoming entirely ready to have God remove our character defects and to walk in the direction of aligning ourselves with our Higher Power's will for us.

Personal Step Six Experiences:

The Seed Store

My sponsor once told me a story about a shop where I could get my heart's desire. She said that everything was available there. I thought, "Oh, wonderful." Then she described her experience of entering the store. She found her heart's desire but, of course, there was a price. The SEEDS of her heart's desire were available; however, she had to purchase the seeds and then plant and nurture them. Only with her continued effort and payment in time and energy would the possibilities become her reality.

At that time, I wanted to have a husband and children. I said that I was willing to pay any price to have a family. My sponsor suggested that my price might be monogamy, less self-centeredness, appropriate boundaries, and a willingness to love and accept with no guarantee of anything in return. "These might be 'prices' you would have to be willing to pay."

I responded, "No! The price is too high."

To be ready to have God remove my character defects to have the gifts I desire in my life, may be a similar price. Is it too high?

Only after years of trying to find easier and softer ways to achieve my personal goals did I agree to pay the prices. Were all the lost years necessary? Could I have had this life earlier? I know that my partner was available when I first heard the story and had the conversation with my sponsor. Finally, twenty years later, I was available. I was ready to have God remove my character defects. I was no longer in the way of God's will for me. I had, however, missed the opportunity to have children.

Can others learn from my example? I hope so. There are prices that I paid for the delay.

Effects of Abuse

"Were entirely ready to have God remove all these character defects." I have continued to hold onto resentments about integrity and betrayal issues. These continue to plague me as I continue to pray for their removal and continue to have opportunities to practice abstaining from the same behaviors. This surrendering is hard work. The clutter, the overworking, and the underplaying are high on my list of things to deal with. So how do I become willing to surrender these character defects and to more and more closely align my life and will with that of my Higher Power? How do I accept the person I am becoming? I have had more experiences of clutter, grudges, and reluctance to let go of old resentments. I cannot let go of them. Integrity and betrayal issues that have connections to abuse as a child are connected. I have written about them. I have shared with others. I continue to strive to do better than I have been. These may really, really, really be God's business as they are not in my power to remove. One day at a time, I let go. I pray.

Step Six teaches me to look at what my character defects are, and I always see many of them that are causing my life distress. I'm ready for them to be taken away, but I don't believe they will be. I'm taught in GreySheeters Anonymous that what counts are actions. No matter what I feel, putting food on the scale and doing GreySheet *no matter what* allow me to avoid listening to my diseased mind and what it tells me. I don't have answers, yet.

Step Six Questions:

1. What does "entirely ready" mean to me?
2. What is a defect of character?
3. What can I do to become entirely ready for my character defects to be removed?
4. What experiences in my life or the lives of others suggest that this task is possible?
5. What is my list of character defects or traits that are troubling me?
6. Which defects of character do I still want to keep and why?
7. Am I willing to add "yet" to those character defects that seem too ingrained to let go now? If so, why not let them go now? Why wait?
8. What circumstances would make me ready to let go of these character defects? Am I demanding that life become that uncomfortable to become ready?
9. What would be the benefits of risking readiness to do God's will instead of my own?
10. What have I already seen in my program life that has made it possible for me to come this far?
11. What am I willing to give up to receive freedom?

Step Seven: Humbly asked Him to remove our shortcomings.

Humility is a vital component of every Twelve Step program. Most of us had struggled for years, relying on our will, before humbly realizing that we were unable to cure the disease alone. The realization and acceptance of powerlessness and unmanageability in Step One are exercises in humility. Humility allows us to seek and develop a relationship with a Higher Power. Each step prepares the traveler for the next step. In Step Two we came to believe something more powerful than our will could restore sanity. For each subsequent step, humility and an increasing depth of intimacy with Higher Power grew.

The choice to seek humility initiates a major change in perspective for most GreySheeters. To humbly come to believe in a Power greater than oneself, to turn one's life and will over to the care of that Higher Power, and then to complete an inventory and share it with God and another person, prepare the way for Steps Six and Seven.

We listed our character defects. No one likes to acknowledge failings. It is a humbling experience, but in working Step Six we became willing to have them removed. Now, with an increased awareness of our character defects, the Seventh Step offers hope and a way out of the despair, depression, and dismay that frequently accompany Step Six. We humbly ask God to remove our shortcomings. We are asking God to match our will with God's will for us.

Many have found that God wants us to be happy, free from fear, and at peace. Others claim 'happy, joyous, and free.' Others speak of alignment with grace and balance. Whatever the description one chooses, humbly asking God to remove shortcomings is essential to attaining the desired outcomes. After that, personal integrity, action, and responsibility are required to live in a new way. Each of us must show the 'Courage to change the things I can.'

Many pray daily a prayer like the following. 'Higher Power, please take the whole of me, every bit, and empty me of self-centeredness, self-absorption, self-delusion, and every other quality that limits my usefulness to You and to my brothers and sisters. Fill me with Your Light, Your Love, and Your Energy that I might better do Your Will. Thy Will, not mine, be done....'

Newcomers ask, "What do I have to do to follow God's plan for me?" Willingness is the key. There are feelings, and there are facts. We ask ourselves, "What is here and now? What is fact?" Being willing to accept what is and then to take the next right step in accordance with what we believe is God's will, is a conscious decision many make each day and sometimes many times in a day.

When we find within ourselves the humility to do what is in front of us; to live with love, kindness, and tolerance for oneself and others; and to grow in acceptance, peace, understanding, and compassion, we are given freedom from our character defects. We begin to see the outcomes of our humility. Humility brings more compassion, which brings more humility as we see that each of us is a part of a large world of humanity living together on a small blue marble planet. Let us remember the view from space. Perspective.

Thus, we learn to live in humility without humiliation. The desire to know and to do God's will was often missing from our lives. Self-reliance led to defiance and excessive pride. Too much self-reliance blocks God out. For many of us, putting down the food was the first experience of surrender as we climbed the steps. Our humble reliance on a Higher Power is indispensable.

"How would a humble person handle this?" This quote was found on the desk of a man recognized as a founder of an organization that created one of the greatest social movements in the 20th century. It is the question of our lives always.

Before coming to GSA, most of us had more experience with humiliation than with humility. Humiliation was a fact of life. It was often one of the reasons we came to GSA. "I felt humiliated by my size. I was embarrassed by food stains down the front of my clothes and by being caught eating," said one long timer.

Since coming to the program, some again felt humiliated when weighing and measuring in public. Others, to avoid weighing and measuring publicly, chose to prepare and carry with them all the food that they needed to eat. One long timer laughed, "I carried everything for almost every meal in my first year and a half. Then I got married, and my husband worked out of state for one, two, sometimes three weeks of each month. I could choose to go with him and weigh and measure my food in restaurants or stay at home. I learned to weigh and measure publicly."

Over time, most GreySheeters overcome any discomfort associated with using their scales in public. They accept weighing and measuring as parts of the solution that work. "I realized that my scale was a small package to carry compared to the insulin, needles, and testing kit my diabetic father had carried. I had the choice. I chose the scale," said a member who is living at a healthy weight.

One old timer explained, "When people were curious about my food scale, I would tell them that I weighed and measured to make sure that I ate enough food for my GSA program. Most days that was true, for only once in a while was the measuring to keep me from eating more than my allotted amount. If the person appeared to want more information, and I felt comfortable in sharing, I would disclose the number of pounds I had lost and my freedom from cravings. I would give the website for GSA. The humiliation I felt when weighing and measuring in public had turned into an opportunity to do service for others and humbly to be an example of the success of GSA."

This bears out what many philosophers and practical people alike have discovered. Acceptance of reality proves to be the antidote to anxiety, fear, depression, and resentment; all of which regularly trigger humiliation. "It is what it is," some say. A philosopher might say, "*Inhabit your body, pay attention to what is, and stop complaining.*" In the program, those words might be translated into the oft-repeated phrase, 'I am abstinent and grateful.'

Often, qualifiers will share that what had appeared horrendous or at some time filled with self-loathing, shame, guilt, depression, and despair could be transformed to be shared with others who suffered similarly. The anxiety that separated one from another could then be dismantled.

If we still hold onto some of our character defects because we love them too much, or they still benefit us in some way, it is suggested that we find the benefit of the replacement for this defect. Can one invite a replacement so that the character defect might be freed?

One member shared, "Radical changes in attitudes and values may appear to strip away what I thought I was, but what was stripped away was only a facade, a script, or a costume for the real person I am. The process is not easy. When we earnestly strive to do this step, the unreasonable demands we had once placed on ourselves, everyone else, and even on God diminish to become more and more right-sized. We learn to say "Yes" and "No" with clarity and dignity. We strive to achieve balance in our lives and accept ourselves and others compassionately as human beings. "We are all God's kids," says one of our recovering members. Others, who refer to a Higher Power, describe the elegance and simplicity of aligning with that which is and the resulting serenity.

Any problem, shortcoming, or character defect placed in the light of this step can be transformed, as the eating behavior was in Step One. What hinders this outcome? Only a lack of humility. Humility thus becomes a desired commodity: less self-centeredness and more selflessness in Higher Power's service.

Personal Step Seven Experiences:

A Leap of Faith

Step Seven for me is a continuation of the identification of the character defects and the reasons why I need to get humble to ask for them to be removed. It's also preparation for the action of asking these character defects to be removed. I know that I don't have to feel it or even think that it'll work; I just have 'to act as if' and do this. Some call this, "Fake it 'til you make it."

To step from humiliation to humility is a leap of faith. I strive to return to what I am and have always been but hid under facades of FEAR: *'False Evidence Appearing Real.'* I was afraid. Today, I still have fears but when shared with God and others, I have less built up between me and others. What you see is what you get. I strive to *'Face Everything And Recover'* today. What a practice in humility: to be who I am and to strive always to be, do, and become more of what I am and to increase my alignment with Higher Power's will for me. Daily Seventh Step prayer and action make this possible.

My Prayer

How might I serve You, Higher Power? What shall I do to be in alignment with Your will for me? Please take from me every character defect that hinders my serving You and my brothers and sisters. Higher Power, I surrender to Your will for me. Thank you for what you take from me and for what you give to me. Amen.

Step Seven Questions:

1. What is humiliation?
2. What is humility?
3. What is self-centeredness? What is selflessness? What is the balance?
4. How do I achieve more humility?
5. How can I be of service to God and my fellows in GSA? In my family? In the world?
6. What character defects do I currently find most challenging to my serenity?
7. Which of my character defects do others currently find most challenging to their serenity?
8. Am I willing to humbly ask God to remove my shortcomings? If not, why not?
9. Am I holding onto my character defects? If so, which ones, and what benefit do they serve? Is there some other way to get the benefit?
10. Which character defects have I already asked God to remove? What was the outcome? Why?
11. How will I know when my character defects have been removed?
12. Am I willing to share these experiences of change with others? Why or why not?
13. Do I know the procedures in which the alchemists were trying to transform lead into gold? How can I compare this with the transformation of active compulsive eating and food addiction into abstinent sharing?
14. How can I pray successfully?
15. How can humility become a desirable quality?

16. If not now, when will I humbly ask God to remove all of my shortcomings?
17. Last but not least, what do I fear to let go? Might I allow God to be the determiner of whether or not it is removed?

Step Eight: Made a list of all persons we had harmed, and became willing to make amends to them all.

Steps Eight and Nine are the sources of a new freedom. These steps in a real and meaningful way offer us a means to clear away the wreckage of our pasts. In Steps Four and Five, we made a beginning with the lists of our resentments, fears, and sexual dysfunction. While writing and sharing our inventories, a list of the people we harmed and our responsibility for the circumstances of our lives took on a new clarity.

Sometimes with embarrassment, fear, resentment, or pride we shared the past with God, ourselves, and another human being. We then went on to Steps Six and Seven to become entirely willing to have God remove our defects of character and to humbly ask God to remove our shortcomings. Now we are ready to do the next step.

From our Fourth Step inventory, we can make a list of the people we harmed. Are there more? In GSA we say, "We are as sick as our secrets." Striving for health and well-being, the list will probably grow.

Some of us put ourselves on this list of people we have harmed. Few of us could say that we were not harmed by the physical, emotional, mental, and spiritual aspects of our compulsive eating and food addiction.

If we can start the process by forgiving ourselves, could we also forgive others for the harms they have done us? Is it possible that they were doing the best that they could do? A willingness to let people off the hook, just as we quit blaming ourselves, is the movement towards freedom. By accepting others and ourselves, we can begin the 'no blame' path and move away from thinking 'You are at fault, and I am not."

No longer victims, we can take responsibility for our choices. Making the list of the people we harmed is the first task of this step.

Some people choose to make more than one list:

1. Those I have harmed to whom I am willing to make amends now.
2. Those I have harmed to whom I may become willing to make amends soon.
3. Those I have harmed, and I do not know if, I will *ever* be willing to make amends.

The wise sponsor might suggest that 'ever' be dropped. The list or lists might also include a column for the reason for making the amends. Clarity in this column makes willingness more accessible. "What is my part in it?" was a question in the Fourth Step inventory. The answer to this question is often the reason for making an amend in Step Eight. Another column that some find helpful is a one-word personality characteristic that is connected with our part of the particular reason for the amend. These characteristics, might, for example, be self-righteousness, judgments, fear, and lust.

Looking carefully and searching every nook and cranny of our lives, we reveal the shame, embarrassment, and upsets of the past with the clear purpose of identifying those people, institutions, and circumstances in which we either committed an act that caused harm or failed to do something that might have eliminated harm. We make the list(s.)

The desire to clear away the wreckage of our past is what motivates us to do this thorough housecleaning. How can we help others when walking the streets with head bowed?

In what ways have we been self-centered and harmed others with our focus on ourselves without concern for their needs? In what ways have we done the reverse and focused on others to the exclusion of our physical needs for appropriate food, rest, and time for ourselves? Might the outcomes have been resentments and acting out to demand our rights when we were wronged?

When relationships at home have gone awry, have we sometimes taken these same behaviors to the office, school, or workplace and created havoc there, too? We broaden our thinking and ask, "To whom do we owe amends and for what?"

Some of us have stolen and ransacked the belongings of others to obtain the food and money we thought we needed. We may have failed to accept our financial responsibilities, exaggerated costs for our expense accounts, or deceived others to have what we wanted. The people and institutions we swindled belong on our list of those we had harmed.

Sometimes, it is difficult to see our part, because we see that the other person or institution has done us a much greater wrong; however, to walk this new path, we need to focus on our part and become willing to clean up our side of the street, regardless of what others did. With a sponsor, we can review the circumstances to see if there is anything else that needs to be addressed.

If we have been thorough in our list making, we probably will have people, organizations, and institutions representing different time periods in our lives, different locations, and various segments of our personal and professional lives. The list may grow as we continue our process of discovery.

Now with our written lists in hand, we are ready to 'become willing to make amends to them all.' What does this mean?

Let's begin with the end in mind. Our goal is to make amends to 'all' those we harmed. What does it mean to make amends? For some, it is changing behavior. For others, it is fixing an imbalance. For still others, it is making a situation or relationship right. It usually includes accepting full responsibility for our part in a situation or communication that went wrong. When money is involved, it is correcting the situation by repaying the money owed to the person or institution or in some situations when appropriate, as a donation to a third party. In sexual situations, the cleanest amend is often to abstain from the behavior and type of relationship that caused harm and from any similar situations in the future.

The actual act of making amends is taken up in Step Nine, but the consideration of what an appropriate amends might be is addressed in Step Eight. If we tend to be too hard on ourselves, a sponsor may dismiss some items from the list. On the other hand, the list may increase, if when reviewing it with a sponsor, we find that self-justification has raised its head to deny the realities of what we did to others while we engaged in our compulsive behaviors and addiction.

Either way, many of us have found that discussing the list(s) with a sponsor or another trusted adviser has aided us to gain essential clarity. Some amends may be delayed or removed for specific reasons on which sponsor and sponsee agree.

Finally, how do we 'become willing?' By seeing 'our part,' we begin the process. The way ahead may be littered with potholes. "*What if, if only*, and *but you don't understand* are common phrases to erase the need for amends," one long timer shared. "It was always *someone else's fault*," she continued. Taking responsibility for one's actions and choices, without exception, can be as freeing as measuring food without exception.

For those who tend to move in the opposite direction of excessive responsibility and self-deprecation, the sponsor might suggest, "No one can make another person emotionally feel anything without the other being in agreement, at some level." In this case, the list might grow shorter as the maker of the list acknowledges the responsibility to focus on the results of his or her thoughts and actions. For those of us who ate ourselves out of house and home and became destitute and reliant on others, the person on the top of the list might be oneself. Ongoing amends to self as a compulsive eater and food addict in GSA *always* includes continuous abstinence.

Let us review the amends list. Some encourage us to list the names of individuals, companies, or organizations with a one word personality characteristic in another column, the cause for needing to make the amend in a third column, and the attached specific behavior, thought, or emotion for which we are making the amend. This specificity clarifies motives and gives our sponsors enough information to help clarify whether this is an appropriate amend or not.

No matter what the 'list' looks like, once the sponsor and sponsee have discussed it and have modified it, as needed, the parts that are not yet in the 'willing to make amends' section may be taken to a Higher Power in prayer. Sometimes sharing with others the dilemmas and the 'special circumstances' we face with our amends can lead to aid in untangling aspects of the past. Another GSA member's experience, strength, and hope often help us to resolve an apparently impossible problem.

Having become willing to make amends to everyone we harmed, we are ready to enter into a new relationship with God, ourselves, and all other human beings. Willingness and persistence are the keys.

While some people we harmed may still be on a 'No! Never!' list, the fact that they are on a list at all is a beginning. Long timers will say that they have found the willingness to make amends even to some (if not all) of "those" people. Thus, amends occur in time. Willingness to begin and to go to any lengths to maintain abstinence are required. This is a 'no matter what . . . over time' situation.

Personal Step Eight Experiences:

Harm and Pausing

Step Eight is about observation and consideration of where I'm doing harm and to whom and in what way. What I'm learning right now from experiences of others who did and are doing this step is how to know when harm is done and when it is not. I try to seek awareness of what my actions can cause or are causing. In Step Eight I strive to abstain from thinking about possible Step Nine amends. It is important for me to get feedback from another person to see if I'm doing harm and if so, how I can correct it.

I had taken the Eighth Step multiple times before a sponsor stopped me in my tracks. She asked me about my list and then said, "Pause and become willing to make amends to them all." She surprised me. I had never paid attention to that part of the step. I had repeatedly skipped over it, in fact. I was willing to make amends to some on my list; however, my rather long list included a gas company and a few individuals' names that had repeatedly shown up there year after year. When I agreed with my sponsor that I was entirely ready to make amends to them all, I became freer than ever as I made one amend after another. Most I made in person asking at the end, "Is there anything else I need to include? How can I further right these wrongs?" The change occurred in many of the relationships and repeatedly in me. Some amends I needed to do by phone with a script or snail mail with a letter previously approved by my sponsor.

Some say crow is easier to eat when hot; I prefer today to abstain from eating crow cold. I make an amend immediately when I realize one is needed and in the moment whenever possible.

Step Eight Questions

1. What is harm?
2. Have I harmed myself? Others? In what ways?
3. Have I made a list of all those I harmed? If not, why not? What people, places, organizations, objects, animals, sayings, politics, or anything else are on my list?
4. Have I shared with my sponsor this list, including the ways in which I harmed people? With my AWOL group? With another trusted person? If not yet, when?

5. Have I become willing to make amends to them all? (The amends will be addressed in Step Nine) If not, what keeps me from becoming willing?
6. Remembering that willingness is the key, what will allow me to become willing?
7. How does humility play a role in this step?
8. If there are people on my "No! Never!" list, am I willing to remain attached negatively with the same feelings as I have now, or would I prefer these feelings to be relieved with a whisper of willingness? What shift in my relationship with God and my fellows has previously allowed me to do things I thought I could never do? Might those strategies work again?
9. If I am still reluctant, what have I heard others say that might indicate a path for me to increase my willingness?
10. When all is said and done, what do I truly have to fear if I have taken the Third and the Seventh steps sincerely? By looking at my fears and sharing those with another, might I find the means to increase my willingness?
11. What would an older version of myself advise me at this time?

Step Nine: Made direct amends to such people wherever possible, except when to do so would injure them or others.

Step Nine is the step work that precedes the freedoms. It is the last step dealing with the wreckage of past actions, thoughts, and omissions. Future steps deal with the present and its challenges. Step Nine gives us an opportunity to get rid of the baggage of the past. Most GreySheeters see these amends as a direct result of Steps Four through Seven. To reiterate, in Step Eight, we listed the names of individuals, companies, or organizations with a one word personality characteristic, the cause for needing to make the amend, and the attached specific behavior, thought, or emotion.

Some people attempt to complete one amend each day, to finish the task and move on to the serenity and peace of daily upkeep promised in the remaining Steps. Some want to do the amends first on the list from Step Eight entitled, 'Those I have harmed, and I am willing to make amends now.' These members are continuing the 'become willing' aspect in Step Eight. Some are aware that the opportunities to make amends are apparent when the willingness has come. People and circumstances arise to invite or facilitate the amend making. For others, the awareness comes that the opportunity to take responsibility for ourselves has always been available, but the willingness has only recently come to us through Step Eight.

Sponsors or trusted spiritual advisers can help to determine if, when, and how the amends are made. It is wise to discuss the amends with a sponsor to clarify the purpose and the method. "Am I attempting to make the amends to feel better and then continue the same behavior? Or am I truly willing to participate with my Higher Power in the process of amending or changing my thoughts, feelings, and behaviors as they relate to this person or institution?" These are questions GreySheeters ask themselves.

In some circumstances, the sponsor will suggest methods to amend the situation. Each one can learn from the qualifications of others who share their experience, strength, and hope regarding their lives. The specifics they share add to our possibilities and give us ideas about how we might behave in similar situations. Members share that serendipity will provide the opportunity to make an amend; however, when an opportunity does not present itself, a phone call to make an appointment will usually work.

For financial amends, a letter or personal agreement with a schedule of repayment follows immediately on the acceptance of the responsibility for the debt. The certainty to pay in a timely fashion is our agreement with God, the other person, and self. Sometimes the amount paid is small but it *is* regular.

For amends related to sexual issues, a change in behavior is often the most appropriate thing to do. A sponsor will be essential here, as will be prayer and willingness to become what God as we understand God would have us be in our intimate relationships with others. Trust, comfort, honesty, and integrity may be some of the gifts that we receive as we exercise these behaviors in our newly defined relationships. We strive to be and do what God would have us be and do, without exception, in this area of our lives. Setting and holding appropriate boundaries open the doors to spiritual freedom beyond our previous experiences.

In some sex-related circumstances, a sponsor will suggest a conversation with the sexual partner in which one 'owns' the selfishness and inappropriate behavior. Also, we abstain from further harmful behavior and request forgiveness. Whether the other person can accept it or not, 'our side of the street' is clean. "Am I willing to leave it that way?" is a question that each of us must ask and answer in thoughts and actions. Sometimes, the sponsor will suggest abstinence from contact and a commitment to abstain from similar behavior in the future.

A sponsor or another GreySheeter, who has taken this step will surely share experiences how once the work has begun, the changes come. Sometimes, opening the door of communication as the result of an amends made for one person's debris invites another's willing admission. Clearing away our wreckage is the essance of the amends process. What the other does or does not say or do, in response, is not our concern. We are freed from the wreckage of our past life based on willingness and actions.

Occasionally the response we get may be negative. With love, tolerance, and kindness, we move on. Sometimes, we must accept that the other person sees the situation quite differently.

When anger or resentments are involved, the appropriate action is to express willingness to own 'my' part in the situation, without any reference to the part of the other person. What the other person did or did not do is not 'my' responsibility.

When a person to whom we need to make an amends has died, some find that writing a letter of amends to the deceased and reading it to a sponsor satisfies Step Nine. We might also read the letter at the gravesite or another peaceful place and then take some symbolic action. Remembering the deceased person when we are in a circumstance with the choice to act differently can be an ongoing amend. Some have found that burning the letter after taking the time to reflect, pray, and meditate on the situation, also serves as a relief.

When money is owed to a person or institution to which sponsor and sponsee agree that a contact would not be appropriate, then the money is 'paid' to a charity. Still others have sent an anonymous money order equal to the indebtedness to someone who has a financial need that sponsor and sponsee agree would be served by the anonymous funding. This is called paying it forward.

To make amends for harming ourselves, some consider an amendment of behavior and thoughts needed not only in individual changes but also in amending our relationship with God, as we understand God. We ask ourselves, "In what ways have I been less than I could be? How might I better align my will with the will of my Higher Power?"

There are two sayings: "There are no victims; there are only volunteers," and "That was then; this is now." Although these may sound harsh, they mean that while many were victims as children or beyond, intentionally or unintentionally, today we have the power to choose and the responsibility to act wisely, appropriately, and with loving self-care.

Accepting responsibility now for what is happening as a direct result of our current choices and actions is a testimony to growth. "Letting go of the past that I once clung to as the reason for how I am now, may be the most important amend I make to myself," one member commented. She continued, "I was the one choosing to be unhappy in my circumstances. Now I can pray the Serenity Prayer. I can take the actions to change what I can. I can take the actions in thought and prayer to accept what I truly cannot change. I can choose to live in the wisdom of continually seeking to know the difference."

While in the midst of making amends, we ask, "Is there anything else for which I need to make an amends?" Many times this question will broaden the conversation and clear additional challenges. Sometimes the answer allows other amends to be made that open hearts anew.

We must remember that the amends are done "except when to do so would injure them or others." We may not choose to remove our guilt, remorse, or shame by burdening another person with information that does not serve that person. Personal freedom at the cost of injury to another is not a choice we can make. By discussing all amends with a sponsor or trusted spiritual adviser, most situations that might injure another person can be avoided. Prayer and meditation on each circumstance might also aid us in preparation for the amends.

When amends might cause injury to self or family, prayer, careful consideration of circumstances, and close work with an experienced sponsor are essential. Discussion with the spouse or other adult family members who might be impacted will offer additional insights. Taking the time to weigh the effects and to strive to be in alignment with Higher Power's will are essential. The outcome may still be the willingness to do jail time or to acknowledge a large debt; however, the others who might be harmed have participated in the discussion. Prayer and a sponsor's aid are still essential. Preparing a script for amends, reviewing all with a trusted advisor or sponsor and refining the process will often remove the need for additional amends when the initial attempts were botched. "Only fools rush in. Easy does it but do it. Don't do it alone," offers an experienced amends maker.

At this juncture in the Step work, each person has progressed significantly and may agree with the following: We will know freedoms beyond our wildest dreams:

- Freedom from the phenomenon of physical craving.
- Freedom to experience clarity of mind.
- Freedom to eat diversely from a wide variety of delicious and nourishing fruits, vegetables, oils/fats, and proteins.
- Freedom to live in a body healthier than any previously known.
- Freedom to become what each of us always wished to be or someone new.

- Freedom from the exorbitant cost, serious damage, and health consequences of food addiction and compulsive eating behaviors and thinking.
- Freedom to relate to others independently and interdependently.
- Freedom to experience one's own reality.
- Freedom to express oneself clearly and authentically to others and Higher Power.
- Freedom to set and keep appropriate external and internal boundaries, the ones that hold others at appropriate distances and those that contain what comes from inside oneself.
- Freedom to fulfill the potential ignored or forgotten and to become who I AM now.
- Freedom to strive to align with Higher Power's will.

Taking full responsibility for our actions in the past and present we walk forward in freedom.

Personal Step Nine Experiences:

Progress

Step Nine plays an important part when I concretely see that I did something wrong, and I need to correct or repair it. Just saying "I'm sorry" repeatedly are not the amends. It's not enough. Harder are the living amends when I have to change my behaviors, and these are usually behaviors that hurt me the most, not others. It's also not easy to recognize when I'm doing harm or when I'm just playing the movie in my head about the wrong I imagine. Ninth Step work is like all the step work, in that regard: there is always more. Let us progress more, so we grow and change.

Not Perfection

Making amends is a difficult and wonderful process, as I lay my burden down and walk easily into the new day. Making amends means that I may apologize to someone, to give back stolen things or money, to fulfill the promise I've ignored or forgotten, or sometimes just to pray for someone. Making amends has many implications. The amends process gives so much freedom. Beyond the freedoms are the opportunities to not repeat wrong deeds, which means I attempt to change myself and to align myself with Higher Power to become a healthier person in body, mind, and spirit.

Step Nine Questions:

1. When I think about Step Nine, what do I feel?
2. What do I fear?
3. What are my expectations?
4. What am I willing to give up? Accept?
5. What excites me about making amends to others? What surprises me about making amends?
6. How might the amends impact my relationship with family and others? How have the amends changed my relationships?
7. How do I hope that making amends will change my relationship with God and myself?
8. What can my sponsor do to help me with this step?
9. Am I willing to become what God would have me be morally, ethically, mentally, physically, and spiritually?
10. Do I believe that the freedoms are possible for me? Taking one freedom at a time, how has each already manifested in my life?
11. In what way am I willing to share this Step and my actions, thoughts, and feelings about it in a meeting?
12. Have I made my Ninth Step list of amends? Have I made an appointment to review my list and strategies with my sponsor?
13. Are there amends I did not deliver well? Where did I go astray? What can I do differently in the future?
14. Are there times my ego and fear have gotten in the way of my making amends?
15. What steps do I need to take to move forward on the “not yet” and “no never” lists?
16. What were my most successful or most difficult amends?

Step Ten: Continued to take personal inventory and when we were wrong promptly admitted it.

Having worked the first nine steps, we have made progress in clearing away the wreckage of our past and have begun to live a new way of life. In Step Ten, we begin to practice Steps 1-10 each and every day, one day at a time. We eat abstinently and strive to live with increasing integrity. We try to apply the same honesty in all areas of our lives as we continue the practice of weighing and measuring our food. Most of us have learned the hard way that we must take self-inventory on a daily basis to maintain our abstinence. While we are often faced with opportunities to take liberties with our ethics, our morals, and our behavior, we find that we do not have the freedom to do so, any more than we would independently adjust our food measurements. Our abstinence depends on our continued right behavior and spiritual connection.

The willingness to be as clean with our 'creeds and deeds' as with our food gives each of us a life beyond our wildest dreams. First comes the willingness to make our personal inventory-taking a daily task. To succeed in daily abstinence, we must persistently, one day at a time, search for the parts we played in every upset or interaction that caused us discomfort, regardless of how small the upset might have seemed. The collection of little irritations, one after another, leads to the thoughts and behaviors that previously kept us in the food. To continue the same behaviors after we have cleaned house by working the Steps only leads to the soul sickness again. This can propel us back to our previous lives. We learn to watch for these creators of misery - resentment, fear, selfishness, and harming others, either directly or indirectly.

If we continue to behave in our old ways, the emotional hangovers of our pre-program eating can quickly return. If instead, we choose to do a thorough daily inventory and strive to become what we believe our Higher Power would have us be, each of us can acquire, one day at a time, back-to-back abstinence. The past fears, resentments, and impulsive behaviors can be removed in abstinence. We review in our daily inventory the upsets that we used to eat over, and we ask that the underlying character defects be removed. We now strive to live each day in our new way of being.

Inventory assists each person to make peace with that which she or he wishes to be and is in the process of becoming. Each inventory serves to align increasingly the writer with his or her belief in the Higher Power's will. Nothing can so quickly remove obsessive thoughts and behaviors. In GSA, we have come to understand that when we are distressed by something, there is some part we played in the creation of the discomfort, and there is something that we can do to relieve the distress.

"When one finger is pointing out in the judgment of someone's behavior, three are pointing back at me. One finger says I used to do this behavior; another says I am doing it now, and the last says I will be doing it soon!" Abstinence helps!

Some ask if there is anything that is outside personal responsibility? The abuse that we experienced as a child seems to be the only exception. The fact is that freedom comes from seeing our role in the actions of our daily lives. By taking responsibility for our circumstances, we can change and create different circumstances. We must take responsibility for our recovery from compulsive eating and active food addiction. Abstinence serves as the basis of our daily life. This means doing everything that we need to do to stay abstinent. That includes providing foods that we need, having backup scales, planning, protecting, calling and having deep connections with GreySheeters, doing service, asking for help to accomplish the responsible actions, and seeking a Higher Power.

Resentments destroy abstinence. Unmet expectations create resentments. Asking questions to clarify what others are thinking and feeling helps us understand people around us. The fuzziness and fogginess of pre-abstinent thinking and pre-abstinent behavior and commitments can change radically each day by using a simple daily inventory process that cites our shortcomings and attempts to set things right immediately.

The inventory can come in different forms. It may be a spot check immediately after an incident. We ask God to remove the problem, discuss it with someone and make amends quickly. After all, why would we want to carry that around all day?

It is also a daily assessment of our alignment of 'creeds and deeds' or of how closely we are 'walking the walk.' We suggest that daily inventories be read to God and another human being. This does not take long. When done daily, the inventories become shorter day-by-day as the willingness to eliminate having to do direct amends changes deeds rapidly. It is best to make direct amends the same day when possible, or the following day when necessary.

Self-restraint and impeccable honesty and integrity of word and deed become attainable personal goals. Self-esteem comes bit by bit as we change our behavior to be more in alignment with God's will for us. One long timer described the process, "Practicing Step Ten is a means by which the deeds and creeds come to agree. Instead of being different, I am what I want to be. I do what I believe is right. I inventory and make amends daily for those behaviors that are still out of alignment with what I believe to be **T**houghtful, **H**onest, **I**ntelligent, **N**ecessary, and **K**ind (**THINK**)."

Most GreySheeters include a prayer in their daily inventory process. Often used is: "Thy will, not mine, be done."

We make an accounting of the positives accomplished in the day. Were the motives positive, even when the actions did not turn out as desired? If we did act badly, what can be done to relieve and resolve the situation? If our motives were negative, how can we act differently in the future?

In the moment, is it possible to change direction and make an about face without more damage being done? So often a quick and clear apology and a correction of the action done may eliminate spiritual blockage that would increase through a day and night! Each of us has the means to make the immediate about face with Higher Power's aid. Then each one can take the next apparent step to make the situation right for all involved and turn the circumstance over and ask for God's will to be done.

Gratitude for the positives and a sincere desire to do God's will are the means to end each day in a positive way and to begin a restful and peaceful night of sleep.

Some GSA members have formats to write their daily inventories. Some examples follow:

A. Some write shortlists in response to the questions and statements below. Each response is just a few words about resentments, fears, names of people harmed, and amends.

1. I am powerless over my eating, and my life had become unmanageable. It is so today.
2. I have come to believe that there is a Power greater than myself that can restore me to sanity (in behavior, thought, word, emotion, and intention.)
3. I turn my life and will over to the care of my Higher Power, as I understand God.

For each of the items below, I include my part for it is the part that I can change immediately.

4. My resentments today are the following: (fill-in)
   a.
   b.
   c.
   d . . . And the fears that are related to each.

My fears that have no related resentments are the following:
   a.
   b.
   c.
   d. . . .

Any issues related to sexual activity, thoughts, or emotions are as follows:

Any other upsets that seem unrelated to any of the areas above are as follows:

Any other people or institutions with whom I had difficulty today (including the reasons):

5. Now, willingly I turn these over to another person, to myself, and to my Higher Power to be resolved.
6. What is my part in each of the issues listed above, and am I willing to address my part? What are my character defects? I ask them to be removed.
7. In what ways can I turn all of me over to my Higher Power to change me?
8. Am I entirely willing to make amends?

9. In what ways, might I make amends for my part and the outcomes of my behaviors, thoughts, and words? What aspects of my non-verbal behavior, including tone of voice, expression, and gestures, need to be addressed?
10. Am I willing to address my underlying intentions, even when they seem positive?
11. How might I amend my behavior, thoughts, words, behaviors, and intentions to align more closely myself with what I believe Higher Power would have me do? What real steps can I take to be healthier in thought, word, and deed?
12. Did I do service today, and how might I be of service tomorrow?

B. Some members use a daily or weekly inventory that they then share with a step sponsor:

1. How many meetings did I attend this week? (Minimum of three suggested by long timers.)
2. What service have I given this week?
3. What step and tradition work have I done this week?
4. What questions do I have related to any of the above or my life this week?
5. What questions do my sponsees have?

C. Another form of inventory involves answering the following questions:

1. What did I do well today?
2. What didn't I do well?
3. What might I do differently in the future?
4. What resources do I need?
5. For what am I grateful?

D. Three questions written daily (or weekly) might serve as an ongoing inventory:

1. What did I allow to make me angry?
2. What did I allow to make me happy?
3. What do I want to be when I grow up?

Whatever way we choose to work Step Ten, we find that our lives improve when we quickly clear up problems that once caused us to eat compulsively. We have found that the outcomes of ongoing self-appraisal can be very dramatic. The daily success in living we experience can be so invigorating that it drives our desire to do daily inventories. We wonder what else can change and improve today!

Personal Step Ten Experiences:

"Only God makes perfect things" - Peruvian Weavers

My goal is to conduct my life with integrity and impeccable honesty and to work Step Ten each day. Now is it possible to do all of this in one day? No, but many of us have made slow and irregular progress. Abstinence is secured, one day at a time, by honest endeavors to make progress daily. Perfection is not possible because each of us is a human being with human frailties and challenges. Each person is imperfect. In Peru, the weavers of colorful and exquisitely beautiful ponchos include an error in the weaving as recognition that "only God makes perfect things."

While perfection may be out of my reach, I have found that I am given moments when I recognize the improper behavior. It is possible for me to change direction and prevent more damage from being done. Often a quick and clear apology and a correction of my action can improve the situation for all involved. I then turn the circumstance over and ask for HP's will to be done.

Living Amends in the Day

The Tenth Step during the day is teaching me to be more aware of what I'm doing wrong and by being aware of it, I can correct myself because I don't want to deal later with the apologies or corrections of my wrong actions. The Tenth Step helps me remember each day what kind of living amends I am striving to make. Step 10 reminds me that a life well lived is about perseverance in my positive thoughts and choices, because all behavior is born of thought. Step 10 embraces all of my humanity and reminds me that I need God and others and also that God and others need me.

Cumulative Effect

There is a teaching that says my life today is the total cumulative effect of ALL my life's choices, which have generated me here and now today. I am grateful Step 10 gives me a structured opportunity to check in with all the parts of myself to re-align myself if I am going astray or have gone off the beam or have hurt others.

Step Ten Questions:

1. Why is a daily inventory necessary?
2. Why not just do a Fourth and Fifth Step annually or biannually?
3. How am I planning to do the daily inventory (or how I am already doing it)? To whom shall I give it and how often?
4. What is the difference between my daily experiences and feelings and my perceptions and interpretations of these?
5. What themes of behavior do I continue to repeat?
6. Do some behaviors only recur seasonally or at particular times or events?
7. What can I learn from the repetitive experiences and feelings, and what can I do to let go of them to be free?
8. What is the path from Steps One to Four? Five-Six-Seven? Eight to Nine? Surrendering? What do I need to do? To whom do I need to make amends? Why do I choose to make these amends?
9. What is humility? What is self-righteousness? What is a balance regarding Step Ten? How much is enough?
10. What is integrity?
11. How does a daily inventory help me recognize my imperfections while striving for progress? How might I accept imperfection as being perfectly human?
12. What part does gratitude play in daily inventory? How and to whom did I express gratitude and appreciation today, or how do I plan to do it tomorrow? (Written notes, verbal comments, phone calls, gifts, or email messages?)
13. How can Steps Five through Nine be part of the Tenth step? How can I make the inventory brief so that it is useful to me, and still leaves me time to live my daily life?

14. What is it that I am wanting and not getting in my life? Have I asked the appropriate sources?
15. Have I taken steps to achieve what I want out of life? What are the next two or three actions and how/when might I take them?
16. In what ways can I be more authentic? What is the next action I need to take?
17. How can I speak with more impeccability?
18. Are the words I use in alignment with what I say I want/believe/am?
19. Are my deeds in alignment with what I say I want/believe/am?
20. If so, how can I better demonstrate love, kindness, and tolerance for myself and others?
21. If not, what words and deeds can I change toward myself and others?
22. In what ways can I be more truthful today?
23. How did I uplift others today? How can I increase this?
24. Have I tried to check out my perceptions and interpretations with questions like, "Are you feeling…?" or statements like "I'm wondering if…." or "Is it possible that...?"
25. "What would it take to make me willing to change?"
26. How will I know when I have had a successful day?
27. Have my deeds and creeds matched today? Am I learning to say "No" and "Yes" more clearly and precisely?
28. To whom do I still owe amends? For what (my part)? Am I willing to make amends for my part? How will I make the amends? Verbally? With changed behaviors? Always remembering, "Except when to do so would injure them or others."
29. Did I make any agreements today that I do not intend to keep? Did I note each agreement so that I won't forget it? Did I schedule a time to fulfill the agreement? If I had to break an agreement, did I communicate this at the earliest possible time?

Step Eleven: Sought through prayer and meditation to improve our conscious contact with God, as we understood Him, praying only for knowledge of His will for us and the power to carry that out.

In response to Step Eleven, some might say, "What an order!" In Step Eleven, we are choosing to make ourselves available to have a real relationship with the Higher Power we recognize. We do this with a daily commitment to prayer and meditation. Some GSA members experienced momentous growth and development in their conscious contact with their Higher Power. Others discovered that with the time spent, a New Reality developed in our lives. Growth in our conscious contact can be apparent in an altered response to circumstances - a new way of being.

Let us look closely at the three parts of this step: 1. *Sought through prayer and meditation,* 2. *to improve our conscious contact with God, as we understood Him, and* 3. *praying only for knowledge of His will for us and the power to carry that out.*

Some of us came to GSA with a belief in a Higher Power different from what has evolved by the time we get to the Eleventh Step. In Steps Two and Three, we improved the relationship with our Higher Power. In Step Eleven, we introduce another daily practice to align further ourselves with this Power.

'Sought through prayer and meditation,'

We seldom use the word *sought* in modern speech. It means to seek or hunt for something that is desirable in an attempt to acquire it and have it for our own. The object of the search is something that we are yearning to find.

How can we do this? Some adopt a religious practice with which they are already familiar, like going to mass or reading the Bible. For others, libraries and religious institutions offer literature, including prayers and liturgies, which may serve to accomplish this goal. Still others adopt something altogether different from their past experiences. One prayer that has served some members is the *Prayer of St. Francis.* Although St. Francis may not have been a compulsive eater, he suffered from an undisciplined life and came to his Higher Power with the following prayer:

'Lord, make me an instrument of Your peace. Where there is hatred, let me sow love; where there is injury, pardon; where there is doubt, faith; where there is despair, hope; where there is darkness, light; and where there is sadness, joy. O, Divine Master, grant that I may not so much seek to be consoled as to console; to be understood as to understand; to be loved as to love; for it is in giving that we receive; it is in pardoning that we are pardoned; and it is in dying that we are born to eternal life.'

For some, taking action like walking, gardening, or focusing attention helps; for others beginning with a moment of relaxation sets the mood. Sit comfortably and with closed eyes, imagine a place of peace and calm. Then exhale any worry, upset, or self-centeredness, and deeply inhale an attitude of acceptance, gratitude, tranquility, and serenity. Now, Let us consider the St. Francis Prayer:

'Lord, make me an instrument of Your peace. Ask yourself, "What could this mean today in my life? How can I be an instrument of peace? How can I *'sow love, forgiveness, faith, hope, light, and joy?"*

St. Francis then asks God to grant him the ability to console, to understand, to love, to give, and to pardon for he recognizes that in *'dying that we are born to eternal life.'* This request is for the Grace to be relieved of the bondage of self and to be free of the obsession with ourselves that kept us separate from God and our fellows. For some, it is a step out of the darkness and into the Light of the Spirit. Daily prayer is essential to our effort to increase our conscious contact with the Higher Power.

Meditation is the next aspect. When we meditate, we sit quietly without outside distractions to experience this present moment or a presence. Meditation means many things to many people, but it is deep contemplation however we do it. Meditation practices include repeating the rosary (prayer and meditation), the focus of attention, planning the day, sensory perception meditation, chanting, or focus on breathing. Some of us focus while performing regular daily tasks like putting the dishes into the dishwasher or removing them.

Members who dislike sitting still and doing formalized relaxation or meditation may instead choose walking meditations or gardening with centered attention. By observing the environment here and now and how nature is ever changing, we find peace. Walking can be done with such intention as to have no other thoughts. When walking in town, one notices the surrounding houses, streets, trees, and people. This is enough. Whatever works to awaken our spirit is meditation.

Our early attempts at meditation may consist of thirty seconds of relaxation and awareness of a calm, quiet center. This may gradually increase to an hour-long ritual each morning that includes spiritual readings and prayer. Some practices include another period of meditation later in the day or early evening, where we complete an inventory. When invited to do so, sponsors and other spiritual guides will share their experience, strength, and hope. Remember that this is a lifelong journey. Daily practice and a desire *to improve our conscious contact with God, as we understood Him* (the second part of Step Eleven), are the only requirements.

Sometimes our life circumstances are so difficult that we believe we feel deserted. However, if we can start again with only the key of willingness or the prayer to be willing to be willing, the beginning of an improved conscious contact will again become evident. The path may be challenging at times, but there is always a way forward if we seek it.

Our paths were especially rocky when we arrived at GSA. For most of us, the road became even more treacherous once we knew there was a solution, but we still fought it. Finally, having accepted our powerlessness and the unmanageability of our lives, we were pressed to come to believe in a Power greater than ourselves. After all, what else could help us? No Power was our problem. At that juncture and when making a decision to turn our lives over to the care of God, as we understood Him, we began to improve our conscious contact. As we continued working the steps, we increasingly saw the negative impact of our self-centeredness.

We saw the havoc that fear, resentment, and the sex drive caused in our lives, and consequently in the lives of all around us. To gain power and prestige in our homes, workplaces, and in our other relationships, we had repeatedly used our energies in negative ways. To love and to be of service to God and our fellows had slipped off the agenda. If we were to find the peace we sought, we needed a new path. We were ready to seek to improve our conscious and chosen contact with our Higher Power.

Sometimes the paths that we chose turned out to be wrong for us. Higher Power had another plan, which we learned when we became willing to seek a closer contact and to do God's will. One member was determined to accomplish her goals in her career; however, barriers were all along her path. The way finally became impassable. Mentally and spiritually bruised from the battles she had fought along the way, the member began to pray moment to moment for God's will to be done: 'Thy will, not mine, be done.' Knowing in her heart, 'This too shall pass,' helped her address the immediate pain. While doing Steps One through Nine, the member made amends, and her life path changed rapidly. After conferring with her sponsor, she followed her heart, and a new life and path of doing her Higher Power's will became evident.

When we quit fighting and accept what is before us to be done, we become willing to do the footwork and to do whatever it takes to relieve the pain abstinently. Some consistently pray for God's will for us and the Power to carry it out, so the Sunlight of the Spirit can shine within and around us.

Let us continue now to understand the third section of the step: *'praying only for knowledge of His will for us and the power to carry that out.'*

Those of us who found GSA to be a solution to our eating disorders and food addiction believe that Higher Power's will for our abstinence from compulsive eating is to weigh and measure our food off the GreySheet food plan. Our primary purpose is to stay abstinent and to help others to be abstinent and free from compulsive eating.

In what other ways might Higher Power's will for us be sought? We believe that we are to be of service in the world, to adhere to our primary purpose, and to be free of the self-centeredness that has kept us separate from others and God as we understood Him. When we accept our humanity and our connection with a Higher Power, we increase our acceptance of self and others. We become more forgiving and tolerant of the imperfections and failings of ourselves and others. We can begin to accept that our sight is limited, and what we think is our heart's desire today, might have positive or negative effects in the future. We do not know. We do not know in our lives; thus, we do not know in the lives of others. For this reason alone, we learn to pray only for God's will and the power to carry it out.

Our members connect with their Higher Powers in different ways. Some members pray for specific goals, for other people, or any other concerns they have. With our prayers, we strive to bring forth courage, compassion, wisdom, and life energy while we strive to see what actions we need to take.

The physical power or energy to perform a task is one aspect while the emotional, mental, and spiritual powers are others. What do we need to continue? The answers come when we are steadfast in attempting to bring our will into alignment with God's will. When all else fails, we can ask for a moment of quiet and pray the "we version" of the Serenity Prayer:

> *"God, grant us the Serenity*
> *to accept the things we cannot change,*
> *Courage to change the things we can,*
> *and the Wisdom to know the difference."*

Step Eleven Personal Experiences:

Focusing

In childhood, my feeling for God was devotion and trust and later doubt and denial. Now I behave mostly "as if" in different forms and intensities. It somehow works this way.

My prayer is my speech to my Higher Power, mostly asking for help, answers, or inspiration or turning over my problems and experiencing the benefits of relaxation, tranquility, or serenity. I open the mind and connection to the Universe. I pray daily, but not systematically. Prayer and meditation are included in many actions. When anxious, I meditate more, but many times I am overwhelmed and not able to concentrate on meditation at all.

The experience of HP for me is focusing on the fact that somewhere outside, power exists for all actions, and all the answers to my questions reside. All the knowledge I need is not available to me, but I can invoke some through prayer and meditation.

To deepen my conscious contact with that means more praying, with more meditation, more study and connections with others in recovery, and asking to know what is the next right action. Through that, I am more peaceful, have more trust, feel safer, and feel okay with myself.

God is Everything or Nothing

I was one of the spiritually bankrupt or perhaps more accurately, spiritually wounded when I came into recovery. 22 years later, I can affirm without a shadow of a doubt that working this step with the clarity of GS abstinence has graced me with a transformation of mind, body, and spirit - a conversion of the heart. I now have an understanding and a personal experience of the proposition "God is everything or nothing."

I regularly affirm that the power of God is infinitely more powerful than the power of any other force, inside or outside of me, including food addiction, which is why I remain one day at a time a keen, hope-filled, and grateful student on the path of 12 step recovery.

Conscious Contact

What is important in Step Eleven is the word 'conscious.' "We sought through conscious contact" means that I don't have to wish for something abstract or feel it. Instead, I consciously choose to have faith and to do the actions of prayer. I don't see the part of "praying only for his will" to mean that I never am allowed to express wishes, desires, or concerns while praying or during daily life. Chanting for my goals and the willingness to do the actions to achieve them and chanting for others are important because it is normal to wish, to have desires, to have fears, and to have feelings. When actions support the prayers, HP's will shows up. I'm doing the actions, and the outcomes are not always in my power.

Seeking in my Daily Life

The key word for me in this step beside God is 'Sought,' which means to me that I must constantly seek God in my daily life. I must always be searching for God's will for me. I must practice prayer and meditation to keep and improve my contact with God. I must never stop trying to improve my conscious contact. If I am to stay abstinent and sober, I cannot rest on my laurels because self-will destroys my relationship with God and ultimately my abstinence and sobriety too. If I am seeking and trying, then I do not give in to my false childhood beliefs that God does not love me so why bother. I abstain from those thoughts. The only cure is continuing to listen to God and look for God in everything. God is everything, or God is nothing. I choose to believe that God is everything.

When a Higher Power is Not Named God

I came to the program with names for my Higher Power (not named God.) Occasionally in the group as a shorthand term, I would use the term G-O-D, which to me meant Good Orderly Direction. Other times, I would think of the Powers of Creation within the Universe or the Sunlight of the Spirit. Others with whom I shared spoke of Suffering and Loving Kindness and Wholeness. Higher Consciousness was another name some friends used. Integration and Welcoming were 'names' others identified as helpful to their understanding.

Who gets to name "God as I understand Him"? I do. For me, the name and concept changed over time. The Western Exterminator God I exchanged for a more loving presence and then changed again in my conception to a spiral and when I changed, my naming of 'that which is' changed too. I have a power greater than myself that has hundreds of names. Do I believe that has changed reality or only my perception of reality? I suspect it is the latter.

The child grows and changes and the relationship with the parent changes over time. So it is with me and my naming patterns for that which is: I change and the appearance and my understanding of that which *IS* changes. Did it change? Probably not one bit.

Do I need to use the same name to share a belief with others that something greater than myself is in the Universe? Probably not. We can share without using the same name for HP. Some describe it as outside, and some say it is inside. Others say it is inside and outside. It just IS. The name is up to each person.

Step Eleven Questions:

1. What have I previously experienced as my relationship with my Higher Power?
2. What is a prayer?
3. What is meditation?
4. When and how do I practice prayer and meditation?
5. What is a *'conscious contact with God'?*
6. How do I improve my conscious contact with a Power Greater than myself?

7. What does it mean to 'pray only for knowledge of God's will for me and the power to carry it out?'
8. What are the benefits of prayer and meditation in my life?
9. What does it mean to feel 'more belonging?'
10. What does it mean to be of service?
11. In what circumstances have I felt the intuitive awareness that seemed to be God's will for me?
12. Have I ever experienced or known of others who misunderstood or mistook God's will? How can I avoid misunderstanding God's will?
13. How do I know when I am or am not in alignment with God's will for me?
14. What does it feel like to have the Power to carry out God's will?
15. What is relaxation, and how is it related to prayer and meditation?
16. How can I improve my daily conscious contact with my Higher Power?

Step Twelve: Having had a spiritual awakening as the result of these steps, we tried to carry this message to compulsive eaters, and to practice these principles in all our affairs.

Step Twelve is the 'Pass It On' Step.

Let us look at the four distinct parts of this step: 1.*Having had a spiritual awakening*, 2. *as the result of these steps,* 3. *we tried to carry this message to compulsive eaters, and* 4. *to practice these principles in all our affairs.*

What does '*Having had a spiritual awakening*' mean? Some GreySheeters have had a single extraordinary experience of personally relating to a Higher Power, which forever transforms their personalities and belief systems. Others have had experiences that were gradual and took place over months and years. The combined incidents nonetheless led to a spiritual awakening and a changed life. How do these awakenings occur? They are the result of diligent effort working the Twelve Step program of GSA. For some, the transformation is the change from compulsive eater to one who commits and eats GreySheet abstinent meals one day at a time for decades.

Some members have said that a spiritual awakening is 'a' result of this work. 'A' result would be a spiritual experience, one of many results of GSA abstinence, but this is not the wording of the Twelfth Step of recovery. It says that a spiritual awakening is ***the*** result of these steps, one unique outcome of GSA abstinence. All other outcomes flow from the unique spiritual awakening. Body, mind, and spirit are transformed. The cumulative effect of working the steps is a new clarity of thinking, freedom from limitations that had previously bound the person to victimization and identification with the past. A bonus is an emotional stability and freedom from self-centered fears and insatiable hunger. As a consequence, relationships with self, others, and a Higher Power are enhanced.

'As the result of these steps' is a phrase that indicates the steps are the means to a spiritual awakening. Completion of the steps, however imperfectly, creates the spiritual awakening.

Our individual stories include our experience, strength, and hope. We learned lessons from our initial surrender with Step One and our frequently tearful and angry acknowledgment of powerlessness over a disease that warped our thinking, alternately inflamed or numbed our emotions, and ultimately, if left untreated, destroyed us. Most agree that this disease is progressive and fatal.

Our lives had become unmanageable; however, Step Two allowed us a means to come to believe in a Power greater than ourselves that could restore us to sanity. If then we were willing to turn over our wills and our lives to the care of the Higher Power in Step Three, we could continue the process of discovery. In Step Four we inventoried every nook and cranny of our past to assess the positives and negatives. In Step Five we shared the inventory with God, with another human being, and with ourselves. This allowed us to move out of our imprisoning isolation. Steps Six and Seven gave us the opportunity to look less fearfully at our shortcomings and to ask God to remove our character defects. In Steps Eight and Nine, we had the opportunity to become willing to make amends and then only to make them in a way that would not cause harm. In Step Ten, we outlined a daily method of housecleaning that allowed us to keep current in our step work. Prayer and meditation practice in Step Eleven gave us a closer relationship with the Higher Power. Step Twelve enabled us to share with others what has so generously been given to us. Paradoxically, we get to keep what we are willing to give away.

'We tried to carry this message to compulsive eaters....' In another Twelve Step program there is a story about the death of one of the founders. There was a Swedish ivy plant at his bedside. The founder's wife took it home and when people came to offer condolences and asked what they could do, the bereaved woman snipped off a piece of the plant and suggested that they, "Pass it on." So it is with this step.

In Twelve Step work, we have the opportunity to become the messenger of recovery. By being abstinent in GSA and working the Steps, we have been changed in every conceivable way. We carry the message through our altered way of living and by freely sharing with others what has been given to us. Our most shameful experiences transformed into stories that showed other sufferers that they were not alone. Not one of us was unique. Having worked the steps, we saw that we are all more similar than dissimilar. By sharing our experiences, we were freed from their shameful hold and could help others to see that we are all brothers and sisters.

The work of the Twelfth Step may be making coffee or setting up chairs; opening a meeting place each week; being present at a meeting to be available to share with another compulsive eater or food addict; starting a meeting; serving as a group's trusted servant; being available to share on a personal, group, intergroup, national, or international level; doing a part in GSA intergroups; or serving as a delegate and committee member in the GSA World Services Conference. In whatever capacity we serve, our primary purpose is to stay abstinent and to carry the message of recovery to those who still suffer from compulsive eating and food addiction.

We find the confidence and capability to do these things by doing the Steps ourselves and by relying on a Power Greater than ourselves. Our dependence on a Higher Power frees us to experience new attitudes and new willingness to be of service to God and our fellows. We know that justice, compassion, forgiveness, and love support each of us at all times. The realization that we are not in charge allows us to expand our humanity and spirituality. We learn to be more focused on what we can give, instead of what we can get. We learn how we can understand instead of always trying to get other people to understand us. We change our focus from protecting ourselves to loving Higher Power, our fellows, and ourselves.

This frees the creative energy that we wasted in the past. We find we can now concentrate physical, spiritual, mental, and emotional energies on their real purposes. While we may have used our abilities to harm ourselves and others in the past, we are now free to help and heal. Do we do this by shouting our GSA membership from the rooftops? Many of us have done so early in abstinence. Later, we discovered that by staying abstinent, one day at a time, by working the steps in our own lives, and by sharing our experience, strength, and hope with others, we open channels of opportunity to serve God and our fellows. By letting go of compulsiveness and self-will, we allow our talents to be used. We continue to strive to align our will with God's will for us. We pray and then we do what is in front of us to do to stay abstinent and help another compulsive eater or food addict. When life is hard, we know from experience that 'when all else fails, working with another compulsive eater or food addict will help each of us.'

Anonymity is a spiritual gift that we honor. We maintain members' anonymity, which enables newcomers and all of us to feel safe and free to strive to obtain and maintain abstinence. By breaking our anonymity, when it is appropriate, we offer the possibility of a recovery to the compulsive eater who still suffers. One longtime member of GSA illustrated this, "In answer to questions about my scale in restaurants, I say that I weigh and measure my food because I am a member of GreySheeters Anonymous, a Twelve Step program for people with sensitivities to grain and sugar." The inquirer may have a family member who needs this program or may be curious about it himself.

Our tradition regarding press, radio, and films further addresses anonymity. Humility and anonymity go hand in hand. In what circumstances and for what purpose is the sharing of GSA membership and success? Is it prideful or is the purpose to serve others? Each has the right to share his or her membership in GSA, except in press, radio, or films; however, no one has the right, unless specifically given, to break another's anonymity.

In Step Twelve, how do we "*practice these principles in all our affairs*"? Some have identified a particular principle for each step. Other members list the principles as abstinence, honesty, love, trust, tolerance, kindness, humility, serenity, faith, self-examination, clarity, restitution, forgiveness, integrity, commitment to service, and willingness to continue to strive to grow. No one does any one of these perfectly in each and every area of life. The point is that we are willing to grow spiritually. We do not expect perfection. We strive for improvement and progress.

From the newest newcomer encountering Step Twelve after completing step work through sustained efforts, to the 25-years-abstinent member who finally completed a thorough inventory and the subsequent steps, the Twelve Steps open the door to recovery. Sometimes the paths we choose to take may be rocky. We now know that we can always retrace our steps or find a new path. We are never alone. We who travel together in GSA know that our Higher Power, whatever we choose to call it, is with us always, in the darkest and most glorious of times. We pray that each of us may continue to be abstinent and to practice these steps that encourage continuing growth, one day at a time. As we remember our primary purpose is to remain abstinent and to carry the message to those who still suffer from compulsive eating and food addiction, let each of us pray: "*God, grant* ***us*** *the serenity to accept* *the things we cannot change, the courage to change the things we can and the wisdom to know the difference."*

Step Twelve Personal Experiences:

Life Guide

My life has been changed by these steps, which I try to live in all my affairs. I've got the power to face reality and to solve or accept life problems one by one, step by step. The GSA Steps enabled me to accept others and myself, with limits, growth, and changes as well. I became more responsible towards my life and recovery, not just waiting for something to happen or somebody to solve the problem for me. These Twelve Steps are a crucial life guide for me.

Nowhere and Now Here

The emotional and mental balance and clarity that flow from GreySheet Abstinence allow me to share my experience, my strength, and my hope authentically, instead of only the theory behind each step. I have learned to carry the message and not the mess, which as an overly responsible offspring of an alcoholic has been a challenging and freeing blessing. I have learned to carry myself with grace and gratitude to a God I thought bitterly was NOWHERE, but the collective you showed me was NOW HERE in this present abstinent moment.

Essence: Carrying the Message

The essence in Step 12 is trying to carry the message. For me this means first of all trying to carry the message of GSA abstinence and everything that the program we do involves: from steps to service and changing life altogether while staying abstinent and continuously striving to work the program and do what is good.

Step Twelve Questions:

1. What is a spiritual awakening?
2. Have I had one? If so, when?

3. Was my spiritual awakening of the momentous occasion variety or the gradual change variety? How would I describe my experience(s)?
4. What has been the effect of taking the Twelve Steps?
5. What message do I carry to the still-suffering compulsive eater and food addict?
6. What message would I like to carry? How might I get from here to there?
7. What is anonymity, and how is it related to newcomers and their needs? To long timers?
8. What is *trying to carry the message?* And for what am I responsible?
9. In what ways might I be of service?
10. How much service is necessary? How do I find balance in my life?
11. What are the principles of the Twelve Steps of GreySheeters Anonymous?
12. How do I *practice these principles in all my affairs*?
13. Is there any part of my life that is off-limits to the steps and principles of GSA? If so, how can I ask for even that area to be open to the program?
14. How can I open my heart to others and share the abundant gifts of abstinence?
15. How much is 'enough' concerning steps, gratitude, and practice of these principles in all my affairs?
16. Am I passing it on? In what ways can I model service for others? Do I discourage the service of others? How might I abstain from that?
17. Have I had a spiritual awakening as the result of these steps? If not, which step(s) do I need to address?

GreySheeters Anonymous
TWELVE TRADITIONS

Tradition One: Our common welfare should come first; personal recovery depends upon GSA unity.

In GSA, we have learned that we must weigh and measure our food, without exception, to be abstinent. For us to be able to stay abstinent, we need GSA unity. We need to focus on our common purpose: to abstain from compulsive eating and to help others to achieve abstinence. We need to abstain from behaviors that lessen the loving, supportive, and spiritual atmosphere of our Twelve Step community. It is in our community that we gain abstinence and thrive, one day at a time.

What is our common welfare and why should it come first? We cannot achieve GSA recovery alone. We need to be sponsored. We need to sponsor. We need the community of GSA to sustain and support our abstinence. This is equally true whether we are in a location where many GSA members live or alone in an outpost, a town or region where the GreySheeters are too few to have live meetings. We need the Fellowship to remain strong and united so that we can carry the hope of recovery and a program that works to those who suffer from compulsive eating and food addiction. Participation is the key to unity.

There are many ways to participate actively in our organization. In meetings, we can serve by reading the Preamble, the Steps, Traditions, and Conference Approved Literature. We can aid recovery by regularly attending and contributing to face-to-face and phone meetings, round-ups, and retreats. We recover by working the Twelve Steps with a sponsor or in A Way of Life Group (AWOL). We can give away what we have been given in many ways. We serve as speakers, leaders, treasurers, bookers, moderators for the Phone Bridge, and leaders for Recovery from Relapse Meetings.

Each registered Group has a General Service Representative (GSR) who participates in an Intergroup. The Intergroup includes a chairperson, secretary, treasurer, a delegate to the World Service Conference, and GSRs from either a geographic area or from a group of Phone Bridge Meetings. Additional ways to serve include as a delegate to the World Service Conference, as a member of the GreySheeters Anonymous World Services (GSAWS) Board of Trustees, or as a member of the GSAWS Committees: Conference, Literature, Public Information, Legal, Finance, Archives, Communication, Nominations, Structure, or Bylaws. Participants or moderators in other internet services, sponsors, members who make outreach calls, members who post letters, outpost members who list themselves on the web, and web servants provide service to the GSA community. Members serve GSA by creating conferences, retreats, or new meetings. Members and potential members who are sponsees or receive outreach calls and letters also serve by accepting the service of GSA members.

Meeting attendance is important to our unity. Each meeting is different. Some meetings focus on literature while other meetings have speakers who share their personal experience, strength, and hope. Some meetings are topic-focused speaker-discussions while others concentrate on the steps and traditions. Regardless of the type of group, our common purpose is to help the compulsive eater who still suffers and to share the basics of recovery with newcomers. We do this while we continue to eat our three weighed and measured meals each day from the GreySheet. We commit our food to a sponsor, eat nothing between meals except water, diet soda, coffee, or tea, and remember that our GreySheet abstinence is the most important thing in our lives, one day at a time. We share our mantra, a declaration of defined abstinence. Each of us can learn to participate in meetings in loving and appropriate ways. We learn to share within the boundaries of time and topic agreed upon by the group conscience. We learn to be respectful of others, whether they are newcomers or long timers. It is essential to hear newcomers sharing who keep the program 'green' for all of us and remind us where we came from. We also need to hear members with long-term back-to-back abstinence share how they acquired their many days, one day at a time. Their experience, strength, and hope aid everyone in gaining the perspective and wisdom that come over time with continuous abstinence. By sharing the GSA program and the individual's experience of GSA in positive GreySheet pitches, the unity of GSA is maintained.

No matter what group or groups we attend, the unity of GSA and our common purpose hold us together to enable us to continue to carry the message of GSA recovery to any compulsive eater or food addict who still suffers and to those struggling in the rooms, on the phones, or on other media. One day at a time our shared recovery program unifies us as a collective of individuals and as meeting groups with a common purpose.

If individuals choose purposefully, or by mistake, to disregard the Traditions, each GSA member is responsible for sharing in a loving and kind way the importance of our Traditions. We do so to survive as a community of people with a shared program of recovery. We are not alone. As our GSA community expands, and we grow in recovery, we are now able to see the important benefits of the Traditions. We see how they function within our Fellowship and in our daily lives with families, friends, and colleagues.

Groups have faced common problems throughout the history of the GreySheet. Some of that history is now in the literature of other Twelve Step programs that preceded GSA. In recent years, the Twelve Step Program of Recovery called GreySheeters Anonymous World Services has gained experience of its own. We have experienced situations in which Traditions were disregarded, and the well-being of the GSA Fellowship was in jeopardy. Fortunately, members worked to restore peace in meetings, in service, and within the organization as a whole. We all continue to grow as we continue to see the Traditions in action. The Traditions guide us in the GSA Fellowship, in our lives in GSA groups, and in groups outside GSA. Members have suggested that the Traditions are suitable for marriage and business partnerships, as well.

In Tradition One, as in all traditions, we learn how the principles could apply to our relationships at home. A member reports, "I heard married partners share the use of the Twelve Traditions in their home, but, I had forgotten the part on unity. To have unity in our home, each person has to have a voice. It wouldn't work if one person were in charge and controlled all decisions. I need to learn to listen, share, and accept. Other people have the right to make their choices and to choose their actions. They also handle their decisions and outcomes."

Another member shared a similar experience. "As a person who was 'in charge' at work, I had taken many liberties in decision-making in my GSA meetings and at home. I had to learn a different *modus operandi* to be comfortable in a unity-focused meeting and at home. I no longer want to be at odds with my fellows in GSA or with my spouse. No one person's needs or thoughts should force a group or married couple to take a certain action."

"At home or in a meeting, we do not need to take anything personally. We can state our opinions and let the results be in God's hands. We do not need to force anyone or anything to be a particular way. Unity is the meeting's common purpose and our love within our home are two areas in which we can practice daily the principle of Tradition One. Each is one amongst members of the group. Each is one in marriage. The essence of this tradition is the maintenance of a calm spirit free from rancor and animosity. Each handles doing his or her share."

Sometimes newcomers speak outside of the parameters of our 'positive pitches on GSA recovery.' Early in recovery, newcomers may be unaware of the important role of expressions of gratitude in our Fellowship. In these circumstances, sponsors or more experienced members gently offer to hear a newcomer one-on-one after the meeting to give the newcomer an opportunity to grow within the context of shared experience, strength, and hope and to individually share the recovery process in GSA. Service to support our common purpose can be given in many ways.

Members' experience, strength, and hope are shared in meetings and the online groups. Conference-approved literature (often called CAL), prepared by the Literature Committee, is shared experience, strength, and hope written and published by GreySheeters Anonymous World Services (GSAWS) for the use of the Fellowship as well as the public at large.

What members read in their own reading time is personal and becomes part of the individual's experience, strength, and hope. Information about members' readings can be included as part of their experience; however, frequent references to our Conference Approved Literature create a harmonious experience of our shared welfare.

Our spiritual Twelve Step program encourages our group's well-being to become the central focus of practicing 'these principles' in all our affairs. Even though we do encounter conflicts at times, the Traditions and our experience of the group conscience consistently bring us back to focus on our common welfare.

Our GSA Declaration of Unity and Responsibility states "We share the message and service of GSA with the world. This we owe to the future of GreySheeters Anonymous: to choose to act for our common welfare first. GSA's unity supports us and those who arrive next. For this, I am responsible."

For GSA to be and remain successful, we must be united. There must be unity of purpose and unity of execution of that purpose. "Staying abstinent and helping the compulsive eater who still suffers to attain and maintain abstinence" is our purpose. We want to be an attraction to others who might join us. There is usually nothing attractive about infighting, gossiping, and bickering. On the other hand, unity with a common purpose attracts others. For unity to exist, service is essential. We have the opportunity to rise above our differences to serve our common purpose.

Tradition One Personal Experiences:

A Couple

The most challenging parts of relationships are these: our common welfare and the focus on unity. In my relationship with my spouse, I continue to seek the balance amongst dependence, independence, and interdependence. Each of us had a history, and acceptance is the answer to that: acceptance of who I am; who my spouse is; and who we are as a couple. Focusing on the unity of our relationship invites the following: acceptance, love, kindness, a willingness to grow and change, hopefulness, helpfulness, detachment with love, and increasing acceptance. It is essential to remember that the unity of our relationship is important if we want to maintain our relationship on an ongoing basis.

Worldwide Community

I'm grateful to have a worldwide community supporting me in my abstinence. It makes me feel very secure to know that there is someone who has been through every "No Matter What," and if I need guidance or assistance to navigate a situation or event abstinently, all I have to do is ask.

It is very easy for me to endorse Tradition One in larger groups. It's easier for me to step back and accept what the majority is agreeing on. I'm less emotionally intimate with a larger group; it's not a personal issue. I feel the same way at work. Brilliant people surround me. It's easy for me to put my personal feelings aside and listen to all of the information. I feel empowered by my supervisor to share my experience, feel that I am being heard, and know that my opinion is valued.

When it comes to my marriage, there are two of us. I came from the school of hard knocks and felt like I learned EVERYTHING and know what's best for both of us. I understand this about myself, so I try to take the time to pause and listen to my husband without any judgment. I share my experience with him, and we don't make decisions until we are both unified. It's sometimes a bumpy road getting there.

Many in Body; One in Spirit

Unity does not mean that I'm the same as another person or that I feel, think, or have the same opinion or view. I can even be in conflict or resent a certain person or have troubles with other personalities. This often happens when I am deeply involved in service. With all these different opinions, I have to remember that we have the same purpose: to stay abstinent and help another person achieve and maintain abstinence. In Buddhism, they have an expression: many in body; one in spirit. I see unity as having the same goal; although, different views exist about how to do things. We are different personalities with different experiences and behaviors; however, we are one in the shared GreySheeters Anonymous spirit.

Fire Ants Offer Example

Our common welfare comes first: Is my focus 'the group' or 'my will' or the more subtle version of the latter: 'my wisdom, which the group should follow because I know best.' Am I putting my selfishness and self-will aside and focusing on our common good? Am I pulling GSA 'seniority' and urging that it is 'my way or the highway?' Am I focusing only on my abstinent time or on whatever might help each of the group members maintain or attain abstinence? Do I remember that I need the other GSA members and that they need me? Can I see the wisdom in moving forward jointly and not as a 'lone wolf'? Do I remember God is in charge and not me?

I believe the collective intelligence of the group can outsmart the killer disease - food addiction. Acting together for a common purpose on the basis of decision making, not my will, but Higher Power's will for us, we create a greater mind than the one that exists inside of any single GreySheeter's body. We benefit from the wisdom of many in unified action. This experience is not extraordinary but merely replicates that in the remainder of the world where "swarm intelligence" outsmarts predators and ensures the longevity of all the members of the group.

I was transfixed by the fate of a nest of fire ants threatened by rising flood waters. No action was taken by the strongest to look out for themselves without thought for the weakest. None stranded and abandoned. Instead, the ants made a life raft from a mesh of their interconnected bodies and used their precious pupae cargo, their next generation, as flotation devices to keep them afloat. As they reached solid ground, they morphed into a pontoon that helped each and every one climb onto the safety of the bank. They, their pupae, the Queen and their ENTIRE colony survived by working as a team for the benefit of the colony. Unity of purpose and action created survival for ALL.

Prayer: Higher Power, Please help me stretch out of me to Blessed We.

Tradition One Questions:

1. How can Tradition One be applied in my everyday work-life and marriage?
2. How can I implement Tradition One in my GSA meetings?
3. Without domination or animosity, how can I offer my input to discussions?
4. What does *common welfare* mean in a GSA group and other areas of service work within GSA?
5. What does *unity* mean to me, my group, and in other areas of service within GSA?
6. Do I consider myself open-minded? When and where have I been open-minded?
7. Do I respect the views of others? How do I demonstrate that respect?
8. Am I willing to accept and appreciate others?
9. Am I expressing myself for the sake of unity, or am I more interested in manipulation and control?
10. Am I flexible? Do I 'go with the flow'? (Am I rigid and inflexible?)
11. What positives do I bring to the GSA group? To my family? To my personal relationships?
12. In our groups, do we use a timer to limit lengthy shares and thereby encourage unity and participation?

13. How can I be 'part of the solution' of my group's issues, instead of 'part of the problem?'
14. Am I giving with love? How?
15. Do I listen non-judgmentally to those I dislike or do not agree with?
16. Am I an informed GSA member, supporting my groups, intergroup, and World Service in all of my affairs? How can I become better informed?
17. Do I welcome newcomers in the same manner as my long-time GSA friends? If not, how could I change?
18. When I speak at meetings, am I honest in sharing the good as well as the bad? Do I listen to the wisdom of long-time members? My sponsor?
19. Do I understand there are no rules, but there are suggested guidelines created for the common welfare of GSA groups worldwide? How does this understanding change my participation in GSA? In my family? With others?

Tradition Two: For our group purpose there is but one ultimate authority - a loving God as He may express Himself in our group conscience. Our leaders are but trusted servants; they do not govern.

Who runs GSA? As defined and presented in Tradition Two, a loving God as expressed in the group conscience, a majority vote with the minority heard, and an additional vote when a member of the majority requests the opportunity to change his or her vote, constitute the single authority. This principle of a loving God, expressing himself in the group conscience, has guided our Fellowship from the beginning. The controversy that birthed GSA as a separate organization from its parent demonstrated our need for the group conscience. Our individual character defects and demands might have otherwise spelled out the demise of our fellowship. The group conscience of our early business meetings, even the loudest ones, created the GSA organization and enabled it to grow. The growing pains experienced by some intergroups that started, closed, and then started again, demonstrated that an ultimate authority guided our group conscience. Past fears of the potential failure of meetings ceased when members accepted responsibilities as 'trusted servants.'

As time passed, some long timers moved to new areas and started new local meetings to create communities where they could continue to thrive. That left new members to take on larger roles in their communities, and it meant that some members had sponsors across the nation or around the world. Everyone grew from the experience.

Some members who initially sought service positions as something to increase ego soon found that there was work to be done. These GSA members found their goal was to gracefully and humbly put forth the group conscience or be removed. The traditions of GSA repeatedly held fast the treasured principle of a loving Higher Power expressed in the group conscience. Sometimes the time frame was extended, but this principle always came first.

God and the group conscience are clear in the distribution of donations collected from members and in how the groups decided to have a prudent reserve, the least amount of money on hand for emergency group expenses. Groups and individuals send money to intergroups and the World Service Organization. The essence of Tradition Two is the determination of how best to serve our growing Fellowship's needs. The needs include writing and publishing literature, providing public information, and sharing our experience, strength, and hope with new and old members. We ask ourselves, "How might we best carry the message of recovery from compulsive eating to everyone who still suffers?" Tradition Two and our loving God expressed in our group conscience guide us to fulfill this primary purpose.

This belief that our leaders are but trusted servants is central to our fellowship. As trusted servants, leaders in the fellowship honor this tradition. Our trusted servants do not govern. Moderators do not exceed the responsibilities they have. We are never removed from the fellowship rooms. No one can govern.

Tradition Two Personal Experiences:

Desire for Control

Tradition Two is probably my favorite tradition and is probably the tradition that is constantly of use to me in my personal life, at home, and at work. As a compulsive eater, I have deep-rooted character defects, one of which is the urge to control situations in my favor, a defect that came in handy when hiding my binge-eating or making sure I had enough food to binge on. I also practiced this character defect repeatedly when trying to control my eating with little or no results.

In the rooms of GSA, I learned to accept that my ideas and opinions aren't always the best and that the experience of the whole fellowship was a guide available to me if I chose it. I learned that by trusting the wisdom and guidance of my higher power, I could remain open to hearing my group's conscience and voice. Through the years, I've experienced moments when I felt strong opinions about issues regarding our fellowship and struggled to steer my group in the "right" direction. When I've been able to surrender and accept Tradition Two and subsequently trust in the guidance of a higher power, I've experienced moments of actually hearing another member's opinion and changing my mind as a result. I can express my opinion with humility and openness while seeing other people change their minds as a result.

My experience with our group's conscience has helped me tremendously in my personal relationships, especially in my home. I try to be mindful of the fact that I'm not the only one with a Higher Power and to have faith in our combined efforts to want the best for our family as a whole. When I've struggled in my personal communications with my spouse, I've often been blessed with the Spirit of Tradition Two and as a result been able to hear and be heard. Tradition Two taught me that our opinions and voices are all of equal importance and that no matter what, I can trust in our ultimate authority, the loving God.

Humility in the Organization, in Service, in my Home

We are still in such a new place as a fully-functioning twelve-step program. Some of us have had experience in the traditions and concepts through other programs, and many of us have had none. We are on a learning curve. The Traditions are such a great guide, and there is a call in this tradition for us to have humility.

The face to face groups that I have attended in my area struggle with basics. We have such a small core of people who have long-term abstinence; therefore, the same people are the only ones eligible to chair the meetings and be treasurer. We can dream of the time when our fellowship will grow. Paying attention to our Traditions is important from the start. Learning what those traditions are and keeping them foremost in our minds will allow the fellowship to grow and be sustainable. Expressing my gratitude to my loving God for bringing me to this program, for showing me how important the Traditions are, and for helping us to do the service work at the level of the World Service Conference: all reinforce Tradition Two. Remembering that there is a loving God that is expressed in the group conscience allows me humbly to step back when I have a strong opinion that isn't being shared by the rest of the group.

Acting as a trusted servant keeps me committed to doing service, even when it feels inconvenient and uncomfortable. Just as weighing and measuring my food can seem inconvenient and uncomfortable on the surface, if I give it some thought, it is the easier, softer way for me today. I remember what my struggle with food was like, and in that remembering I find the gratitude I need to keep on doing this. I need to know, however, that I am not alone. Service work keeps me connected to others.

Working with Sponsees

I am vigilant about working Tradition Two in my step meetings with sponsees. I am often asked what I think about an issue or a potential character defect at play in a sponsee's life. I always make the point of saying that they should pray and meditate on a particular situation. I never want to put myself above another person, especially one who is already risking vulnerability by sharing intimately with me. God knows the answers, not me. I often smile and say: "I am just another bozo on the bus. God is driving not me. Let's pick up our conversation after you've checked it out with God." I find this works for me and them. I often receive cards and texts signed "Another Bozo." Thank you, God.

Freedom

Tradition Two spells freedom - from attempting to control and from being controlled. This tradition also serves as a reminder that no individual or individuals are in charge and that the group has but one ultimate loving authority, a loving Higher Power as may be expressed in the group conscience.

In another room, I was introduced to business meetings. I made myself stay although my flesh was crawling. I hated the fact that there were people with varying opinions. Being a chameleon, I wanted everyone to agree. That's not life, and it certainly is not authentic. I learned to enjoy the decision-making process. Traditions were followed, and the group made decisions by casting votes. It was sane, and work was accomplished. Sometimes I still feel a twinge when I cast my vote, and it is the opposite of a friend's or does not support what that friend wants to accomplish, but I remember to be true to myself and my friend by being authentic. Group conscience prevails and so be it if my vote is on the 'losing side.' Higher Power is in charge.

Tradition Two Questions:

1. What is our group purpose?
2. How is a loving God the ultimate authority for our group purpose?
3. How can our leaders demonstrate that they are trusted servants?
4. In what ways can this Tradition be demonstrated in our relationships at home and work?
5. What is the group conscience when expressed in a meeting? In our homes?
6. How is a loving God expressed in a group conscience?

Tradition Three: The only requirement for GSA membership is a desire to stop eating compulsively.

Do you have to be GreySheet abstinent to be a member of GSA? Certainly not! The still suffering newcomer, and the member who relapsed are all welcome. Our primary purpose is to stay abstinent and help other compulsive eaters to achieve and maintain abstinence. The desire to stop eating compulsively is the only membership requirement. The means we have found to produce freedom from cravings, and thus from compulsive eating, are to practice complete abstinence from grains, sugars, and alcohol and to weigh and measure our food without exception. We know from experience that following the GreySheet food plan and the GSA program gives each person the opportunity to be free from compulsive eating. We want to provide opportunities to be free from cravings, to be clear of mind, and to live in a healthy body. We want to share this message of recovery with everyone who wants our solution. It starts with the willingness to turn over one meal to a sponsor who guides our recovery.

In GSA, we utilize the GreySheet food plan to stop eating compulsively. We believe that the desire to become GreySheet-abstinent is essential. On the other hand, there is no danger if we invite people who are not yet GreySheet abstinent to attend our meetings. After all, without knowing what GSA recovery is, how will they know if they want to try our solution?

In the challenging early years of GreySheet, only those who were desperate found the GSA community. Other Twelve Step fellowships found the wisdom of complete abstinence as the solution to addiction. In GSA our "complete abstinence" has the definition of three weighed and measured meals each day from the GreySheet, committing food to a sponsor, and having only diet soda, water, black coffee, and tea between meals.

Fears sometimes make us intolerant of compulsive eaters' attempts to find a different solution. Fears that greater public awareness of GSA and rapid growth of the membership might dilute or alter our message have turned out to be groundless, as long as we remember that "It's the food! It's the food! It's the food!" We then weigh and measure our food from the GreySheet without exception and follow the twelve step program. With shared experience, strength, and hope, we are on the path of recovery from compulsive eating.

In our meetings, we announce that "positive pitches on GreySheet abstinence" are requested. Everybody can share in some meetings; in others, minimum abstinence requirements are maintained for speaking as well as leading. Some members and groups ask themselves how to deal with people who are not abstinent and do not want to be, yet come to GSA meetings. One possibility is to designate 'open' vs. 'closed' meetings. Anyone who wants to stop eating compulsively is welcome at 'open meetings,' while only GreySheet abstinent members or those who want to be GS abstinent are invited to attend 'closed meetings.' Whether or not to create this distinction is up to the individual group. It is the dilemma of allowing everyone in and attracting people who are undecided, so they make an informed decision while guarding against dilution of our GSA program or introduction of outside issues. As GreySheeters, our food plan defines what we do. Clear boundaries around what we do and how we do it are central aspects of our program of recovery.

When the use of the GreySheet plan was new, the earliest beneficiaries were compulsive eaters who lost weight. Later, others who were anorexic or bulimic found their solutions in the specificity of using the GreySheet, too. Daily back-to-back abstinence resulted in weight gains or maintenance of their weight goals for anorexics and bulimics. Many members who had other diseases or disorders found that by eliminating grains and sugars and following the GreySheet food plan and by weighing and measuring daily that their other symptoms diminished or disappeared. Some members encountered other difficulties such as artificial sweetener use in the hundreds of packets or tablets per day, chewing packages of gum daily, drinking bottles of diet soda daily, sex and love and relationship addictions, cluttering issues, migraines, alcoholism, prescription and recreational drug abuse, as well as chronic fatigue syndrome, fibromyalgia, Crohn's disease, celiac disease, and polycystic ovary syndrome. Does GSA solve all these problems? No. Nor was it intended to. Each of the people who witnessed symptoms improve came to GSA to address compulsive eating with GreySheet abstinence. Many have found relief from other problems while using the GreySheet food plan, the Twelve Steps and Traditions. By gaining the clarity of mind experienced as a gift of GSA back-to-back abstinence, many have found solutions to their other challenges.

Some members have discussed a change in this tradition to clarify the unique difference in GreySheet recovery. The discussion continues and ultimately the GreySheeters Anonymous World Services Conference, the Board of Trustees, and the Groups will determine any change in our Traditions.

We are a GreySheet community. That is our distinguishing characteristic. If others want what we have, they are welcome. Our only requirement for membership is a desire to stop eating compulsively. This is the starting point for attaining and maintaining GSA abstinence; however, success in achieving back to back abstinence requires adherence to our definition of abstinence using the GreySheet Food Plan one day at a time.

Tradition Three Personal Experiences:

"Don't Wait!"

My journey into GreySheeters Anonymous was a very long one, and I tell all people I meet in GSA and those starting or struggling, "Don't wait until you are 61 to begin this!" I say that because I spent many decades struggling with my compulsive eating and my sugar addiction. I tried every bargain I could make with my Higher Power to hang on to the foods that were keeping me overweight, foggy of mind, and anxious. When I was '12-stepped' and given the knowledge of GreySheeters Anonymous, I resisted even coming to a meeting for five years. Finally, after having many delicious GreySheet meals at my soon to be sponsor's house, I had the insight that would launch me into the rooms. That insight was that I was powerless over my obsession with food, and my life had become unmanageable. I could see the behaviors of a food addict in me. I felt shame, fear, powerlessness, and panic. I made the call for help and started my journey in GSA.

What keeps me here today is still the desire to abstain from eating compulsively, especially when my mind tells me things that place doubt upon my ability to stay abstinent in the future. I respond with the brilliant idea that I am staying abstinent today because I do not want to eat compulsively again. And this third tradition also helps me be kind to the person who may have been my sponsee or sponsor in a prior attempt and who relapsed but tries to come back. Who am I to judge? I need that person, as I need all of us who recognize a solution for our obsessions and compulsions in these rooms. The only requirement for GSA membership is the desire to stop eating compulsively. A blessed statement. It doesn't even mention the GreySheet. It doesn't mention three weighed and measured meals, and it doesn't mention that we do this without exception. That comes with the sponsor. This tradition only states that we need to have the desire to be a member. I'm okay with that.

Coming, Leaving, Returning

At my arrival to GSA the first time, I had a desire to stop eating compulsively. At that time, I was not manifesting the most visible indicator, yet: excess weight. I was not as thin as a twig, but I was not excessively overweight either. When I returned 27 years later, I had taken the 100-pound bite, and I had tried everything to lose it and had failed. I plateaued out at 199 (25 down from my 224 top weight) I was miserable in body, mind, and spirit. Prior to this second time to GSA, I wanted to die.

My first visit, I did not believe that I belonged here even though I knew I was a compulsive eater. I did not want to be here. I was not willing to stay to do the work: the back to back abstinence and the Steps, Traditions, and Concepts. On the second arrival, I did not qualify by the third step definition: requirement for GSA membership is the desire to stop eating compulsively. I only wanted to stop wanting to die; I wanted the fog in my brain to dissipate. I wanted my aching joints to stop aching. My body was unacceptable as it was. The change was not possible. I had tried. I had lost the 25 pounds. I could not lose anymore, no matter what I did. So when did I become eligible for membership? The next morning after one GreySheet dinner, a night of sleep, and an awakening. Then I had the desire to stop eating compulsively because I was without brain fog and achy joints, and I no longer wanted to die.

To continue to have the desire to stop eating compulsively, I had to change. I had to do the steps. I started immediately. Weighing and measuring three times a day demonstrated adherence to the first step. Within the year, I had gotten to the ninth step and contacted an almost fiancé from 25 years earlier and married him 'a minute' after I was a year abstinent in GSA. I completed my first round of the steps. Involved increasingly in service, I had the need to do the work on the traditions and to implement them in my new marriage and in the varied service positions in groups and an Intergroup in which I participated. The concepts came next as I began to work in World Service. I am blessed by this abstinence and the ongoing work with the GreySheeters Anonymous Steps, Traditions, and Concepts.

Bingeing Brought Me to GSA

I met all the requirements for GSA membership when I arrived! I had a desire to stop eating compulsively. I had binged that morning with reckless abandon, furiously stuffing myself and running from cabinet to cabinet. I was completely suicidal with food. I didn't want to live this way; I didn't want to live. I ran from the house to a friend who was abstinent on the GreySheet. She showed me the food plan, took me to a meeting, taught me how to read labels, let me borrow a scale and got me started. FREEDOM! The gates of Hell opened up and let me out! My head was quiet. The struggle was over. I could be a member; I had a BURNING desire to stop eating compulsively.

Members Welcome

When I attend GSA meetings, I remind myself that we all arrived in the halls with the same desire. I look around the room and see newcomers arrive in all different shapes and sizes. I arrived 100 pounds overweight, with one pair of pants that fit. Some people arrive with broken bones from fainting due to starvation. Others have damaged teeth and throats from vomiting or colon/digestion issues from the abuse of laxatives. We're all members. We all belong. We have lost our battles of trying to control food and instead were having them manifest in our bodies in different ways. Our souls are the same at that point: beaten, bruised, aching, sick, and wounded. I welcome everyone with a smile and a kind hello. I make sure each has a phone list and someone to help start abstaining for the first time or to start again. They remind me of my active addiction. I don't ever want to go back, and I don't have to because I am a member of GreySheeters Anonymous.

Last Thing to Try

I learned about this tradition in another food fellowship as well, but it didn't help me become abstinent. I found GSA and knew that this is the last thing to try. If I speak honestly, I didn't even want to stop eating compulsively when I came to GSA. I wanted food, and sometimes I still want it, but the consequences are too dark. I have nowhere else to go except to surrender to this program. It helped me probably also when I started in an area where there were no meetings. I didn't know that relapse or slips were possible. I thought you got kicked out. It helped me to think, "This is the last thing I can try for arresting compulsive overeating." I knew that there was nothing left, so I'd better stick to this or return to the darkness of active food addiction.

This third tradition means to me that everybody who wants to stop eating compulsively can come to GSA. It doesn't say that if you want to come you have to do GSA. Of course we strongly support the use of the GreySheet recovery as this is our path to stop eating compulsively. For me it's good not to have any other option because that means that I'm staying (at least until they invent some pill to relieve me from the obsession. Then I would become a normal eater. Yeah, still hoping for this.) For now, I must satisfy myself with the wish to do GreySheet, no matter what, one day at a time. This is enough of a surrender for today.

What is the Best?

I spoke once with a woman on the phone who had called me to discuss what direction she needed to go as far as food plans. She didn't think the GreySheet was for her. I shared my experience with her and tried to hear her, even though she wanted foods we do not eat. She thanked me for not yelling at her or hanging up on her as some others had.

I don't always know what's best for me, and I don't know what's best for you. But I can ask for inspiration, share honestly, and try to carry the message of my miraculous recovery from food addiction, spiritual darkness, and emotional havoc. This humility has helped me to not be threatened by different ways that people find recovery.

Tradition Three Questions

1. What is the only requirement for membership in GSA?
2. Why has this become a tradition in GSA?
3. How do I demonstrate Tradition Three in the meetings I attend?
4. How do I welcome newcomers and people returning to the program?
5. Do I welcome people who have different experiences?
6. How can I help my GSA groups to remain open to new ideas while maintaining our abstinence from association with any other food plans, systems, or organizations?
7. Do I practice leaving my other affiliations and interests outside the meetings of GSA?
8. Am I considerate and tolerant of others?
9. How might I better practice love, tolerance, and compassion inside and outside the meetings of GSA?
10. In what ways might I practice Tradition Three in my relationships at home, in other organizations, and at work?

Tradition Four: Each group should be autonomous except in matters affecting other groups or GSA as a whole.

Autonomy is the right of each group to make its decisions. Each group has the right to gain its experience, strength, and hope to share in the intergroup and at World Service Conference. Each group can be right or wrong in its actions. Each group may learn with humility from the experiences of the members of the group or others. Responsibility for the consequences of the group's actions goes hand-in-hand with the group's independence. The freedom is substantial, but accountability is intertwined with that responsibility. This autonomy is granted except when the decisions affect another group or GSA as a whole. The group exists within the boundary of the group's impact on other groups or GSA as a whole. As we learn to have boundaries with our food, we also learn to have boundaries about the group and its interactions with other parts of GSA.

Prior to the founding of GSA, many groups of compulsive eaters used traditional anonymous program literature. In some GSA groups, the reading of the Twelve Steps included 'We were powerless over alcohol - and our lives had become unmanageable.' Groups could not agree upon what wording should replace 'alcohol.' The first step included 'food' instead of 'alcohol' when GreySheeters Anonymous was incorporated. That one-word difference was often discussed as the organization grew.

In growing and developing our GSA organization, the attitudes of respect and tolerance were tested. In meetings, some members came and grabbed hold of this Twelve Step program of recovery from food addictions using the GreySheet like those who had preceded them in other Twelve Step programs. Other members continued to seek easier, softer methods to obtain and maintain recovery from compulsive eating. Time, experience, group autonomy, and humility brought us to the organization we are today, secure in our reliance on the GreySheet food plan and the GSA program.

Responsibility to give service in varied situations is always changing and expanding. Those who found the willingness in their hearts and the time to commit to doing service often found abstinence easier to obtain and maintain. Whether a newcomer chose to claim her seat or a long-timer committed to get a new person started or to sponsor, to share on an AWOL (A Way Of Life Group for working the Steps) or to lead one, to chair a meeting, to be a treasurer for a group, to become a booker, or a General Service Representative, a Committee member, a World Service Conference delegate, a Board of Trustees member, a web servant, a moderator, reader and/or writer, a speaker, or an organizer of a retreat or round-up or mini-conference, or sharing experience, strength, and hope as an outreach caller or recipient, willingness to weigh and measure no matter what and to give service were the keys to continued back-to-back abstinence for GSA members. Accepting responsibility to give away what each was so freely given was the means to serve our primary purpose, 'to stay abstinent and to carry the message of recovery from compulsive eating to those who still suffer.'

Trust in a Higher Power and the concept of the group conscience is the grounding for the Fourth Tradition. The self-sufficient nature of each group permits decisions to be made by group conscience. Thoughtful members pray for guidance, vote, and the majority is accepted as Higher Power's will for the group. When mistakes are made, or groups overshoot the mark with their enthusiasm, the wisdom of other groups that were impacted and the Grace of a Higher Power brings GSA groups back into alignment with each other, with GSA as a whole, and we hope, with Higher Power's will for us.

Tradition Four is helping GSA to grow and find balance, just as we have individually, by weighing and measuring our food and working with a sponsor. Autonomy enhances individual and group humility.

Tradition Four Personal Experiences:

Autonomy: The Quality or State of Being Self-Governing

This is one of my favorite Traditions. It relieves anxiety knowing that each GSA group should be autonomous. I like our different styles of meetings, open/closed/speaker/step. Not every single meeting is the same. There is freedom to form groups that will work for the majority of their members. Tradition Four also protects GSA as a whole. It is our responsibility to make sure that we create literature that uses the Twelve Steps and Traditions with permission, as not doing so affects GSA as a whole. It is important that we keep clear records and are transparent in our finances and decision making as this affects GSA as a whole. My GSA group was sending a percentage of our Seventh Tradition collections to World Service. The checks were returned, 'undeliverable.' This affected our group negatively and created a terrible sense of distrust and hurt. Only later did we learn that we had sent our donations to an outdated post office box, and the correct address was on the GreySheet.org site.

We learn as a community, growing and changing accordingly. We all have the opportunity to do service and to give back to GSA what was so freely given to us. We can be respectful and tolerant, but responsible for our actions. We are trusted servants, each of us.

I had the opportunity to serve at the first GSA World Service Conference. I experienced a Higher Power and group conscience bringing people from all over the world together for a common purpose. It was amazing to be in a room from the beginning; figuring out together how to vote, how majority was going to be defined in voting; being patient and kind with each other; listening to different opinions; and experiencing the power of substantial unity.

Autonomy

I had an experience in which people heard only the first part of this tradition. This can be damaging for all of us. I'm also aware of the groups that believe the formats for our meetings are set in stone, even if something else might be better for the GSA member.

We also have to remember that we are a unique 12 Step Program; even though lots of people are in other programs, most of us in GSA could not find our solution for food addiction elsewhere. Our program involves different actions. It is good to look at our meetings and groups to see where we need to be autonomous in a way that we don't negatively affect other groups or the GSA organization. This may be easier said than done. Respect is required. Similarly, for example, in outside situations like work, I can be autonomous but I cannot make decisions that would damage my firm.

A Coffee Pot and a New Meeting Location

This is an interesting tradition. It allows for those who disagree with their groups to get a coffee pot and start a new meeting. It also allows for the group to discover what its needs are and to try to implement them, with a group conscience of the meeting only, not having to answer to any other authority. For instance, I have been part of a group that met in someone's home. There were people who took exception to this and would not come. But for many of us, this was a perfect place to learn about how GSA members deal with their food. As part of the fellowship after the meeting people prepared their meals, cooked, and shared with others, particularly new people. I have seen visitors come to eat and be amazed at the amount of food that was included in a GSA weighed and measured meal. They were introduced to the reality of a GreySheet meal: delicious and abundant. They were introduced to many new concepts while in the secure company of others, weighing and measuring, eating everything that they weighed and measured, and learning different ways of preparing vegetables and proteins.

While adhering to their beliefs, some never chose to come to this meeting. Others were grateful this meeting existed, and it gave them the opportunity to not only hear about GSA but to experience it. If the group had had to answer to a different authority than its own members' group conscience, this valuable experience might never have been available.

At another meeting I attend, the group conscience encourages people to bring their food and eat at the meeting. This meeting is in a room in a church. We do not cook or prepare at the meeting but can bring already prepared containers, weighed and measured, and can eat in peace at the meeting. The reason for this is that some come from work and then have to drive a great distance home after the meeting. We wanted to make it simple for GreySheeters to be able to eat dinner if they chose, without having to go for a longer time between meals. The group chose what it needed for its members to have a weekly face to face meeting and to have the time early enough to accommodate those who still had far to drive both before and after the meeting.

Impact

The second part of this tradition is the most interesting: 'except in matters affecting other groups or GSA as a whole.' That clause is very important for groups having a group conscience because we need to adhere to a sense of unity as GreySheeters in GSA. We have certain precepts that we need to stand by. Otherwise, we could not be a true 12-step program. We use the steps and traditions. We also have very specific directions in that we follow the GreySheet, each of us with the help of a sponsor. If one group decided to make changes to the GreySheet or decided we could weigh and measure *with* exception, then that would affect GSA as a whole. It would sow seeds of confusion in the members who would be given a different message from different groups of GreySheeters.

This Tradition has played a crucial part in several instances in the history of GreySheeters Anonymous. “Each group should be autonomous….” Individuals sometimes translated as “Each group is autonomous.” With no further proviso added. The outcome initially was the continuation of multiple groups with associations and use of literature pertinent to other Twelve Step Programs in addition to GSA whose name the group carried. Singleness of purpose was addressed, and members decided to either leave to create a different fellowship or to stay with adherence to the phrase, ‘except in matters affecting other groups or GSA as a whole.’

Tradition Four Questions

1. What is autonomy? What does it mean for my group? For my Intergroup? For the World Service Conference?
2. What does the following mean, practically speaking, “Except in matters affecting other groups or GSA as a whole”?
3. In what ways might the responsibility and service relationship observed in GSA be applicable in my home group and other relationships or groups?
4. How do freedom and responsibility counter-balance each other in my group, home, other organizations, and GSA as a whole?
5. What does “affect” mean?
6. In what ways might one group affect another group or GSA as a whole?
7. Under what circumstances might I apply this Tradition in my family, neighborhood, or workplace?
8. What are my reasons to use GSA literature? What do I believe the Conference Approved Literature should support? Have I shared my beliefs at the group level? Have I delegated authority to the

GSR to respond to questionnaires from the Literature Committee? What information do I seek in GSA literature?

9. Do I treat every GSA member with respect and tolerance? Whether the person comes to a face-to-face meeting, calls on the phone bridge, calls in as an outreach call, or writes an email, am I respectful, tolerant, and responsible for sharing my experience, strength, and hope?
10. In what ways have I experienced a Higher Power and group conscience together increasing humility, experience, strength, and hope in GSA?

Tradition Five: Each group has but one primary purpose - to carry its message to the compulsive eater who still suffers.

We in GSA have found that what works for us is abstinence, defined in the GreySheet food plan and with our sponsors. We weigh and measure our food without exception, we work with a sponsor, and we continue to thrive, one day at a time. To carry our message forward, we must stay focused on our primary purpose. To dilute the message with outside issues is to doom GSA to failure.

Other Twelve Step Anonymous programs have struggled from time to time throughout their histories with adherence to this concept of doing one thing well. A successful Society dedicated to freeing people from alcoholism nearly two centuries ago was destroyed by the attempts of the Society's members to spread their good intentions into problems other than drinking. The Society lost its singleness of purpose and eventually disbanded over disputes when groups took up controversial social issues. Now this Society is forgotten by history. What can we in GSA learn from that Society's demise?

Tradition Five clearly states that our primary purpose is 'to carry the group's message to the compulsive eater who still suffers.' Our GSA message for the millions of people who do not know that they suffer from sensitivity to grains and sugars, is that only complete abstinence from these substances, one day at a time, can remove the cravings and offer clarity of mind. We have learned that compulsive eaters and food addicts can find freedom from slavery to food by weighing and measuring food from the GreySheet, not eating between meals, no matter what, and having only black coffee, tea, water, or diet soda between meals.

This purpose has a two-fold outcome. The people who suffer and have never heard of GSA will have the opportunity to experience the program. The seed will be planted. An additional benefit of this purpose is that those who share the message with others will perform service and bolster their personal recovery. The impact of sharing their experience, strength, and hope by passing on the message of recovery about the disease of compulsive eating, is felt by both speakers and listeners.

For years, many have recognized that those who weigh and measure their food, without exception, and offer service, whenever the opportunities are available, stay abstinent long-term. Those who carry the message of recovery are constantly reminded of the many gifts of continued abstinence. While sharing the message of recovery, gratitude, and positive attitude, GreySheeters serve as models for others. GSA grows with a positive attitude about abstinence and gratitude as mainstays in the message shared.

Some people who still suffer can be found within the GSA meetings. Life happens to all of us. The feelings that previously caused individuals to escape to food continue to occur, for we are all humans with feelings and life issues. Some of those issues can be resolved by working the Twelve Steps. Much of the 'old baggage' can be relieved and released. The Twelve Steps offer a program of recovery for anyone who chooses to use the Program. As we often say, "GSA is not for those who need it but for those who want it and commit to doing it."

Before GSA, members tried to avoid the experiences of death, loss, sadness, grief, and sometimes even feelings of love and joy. These are normal life events and feelings that everyone experiences. Learning to 'feel the feelings' and to 'let them go' is one of the gifts of abstinence. 'This too shall pass,' is a saying that has been used by many members to allow the moment to be experienced, and then to 'let it go.' "Fake it 'til you make it" serves others. We no longer need to wallow in our feelings and eat to cover them up. We can put on our 'big kid clothes' and move on. By releasing these feelings and their causes through Twelve Step work, members are freed from their old haunts to engage in lives beyond their wildest dreams.

We let go of 'old ideas' that drained our energy. This allows us to experience new vigor and life force. We can use this new vitality in productive ways and share the message of recovery.

The gift that each member receives is a unique opportunity to pass on the message of GSA recovery to those in and out of the meeting rooms. There is recovery from compulsive eating and GSA offers that to anyone who suffers from compulsive eating and food addiction. We can identify with another person who has suffered similarly and share personal experience, strength, and hope. GSA offers the path to recovery and promises a daily reprieve from compulsive eating. Newcomers' sharing helps to keep our memory fresh as to what it used to be like to suffer from compulsive eating and replenishes an attitude of gratitude. We share our gratitude in positive pitches about our Twelve Step program of recovery. By performing the simple acts of GSA daily, we thrive, both individually and collectively.

Tradition Five Personal Experiences:

Carrying the Message

Whether this person is a compulsive under eater, bulimic, anorexic, food addict, or compulsive overeater, I am responsible for carrying the message of GSA recovery - this amazing gift! As a group member, I have this responsibility. When I heard a woman at a GSA Conference make a plea for more public information notices to be in the media so that others might not have to suffer the way she had before even hearing about GreySheeters Anonymous. I realized that the groups in our local area have nothing in the newspapers or health-related magazines, or anywhere else except on the GreySheet.org site.

I had been waiting for public information to get our name out, for someone else to publish a book about GreySheeters Anonymous, and for someone else to spread the word.

Now is the time to carry the message of GreySheeters Anonymous: a newspaper article, adhering to our Traditions of attraction and anonymity, a regularly scheduled informational panel at the library with publicity posted, a regular posting in the want-ads of the newspapers and in health magazines, a post on a website, and placing the "Can't Stop Eating" posters at gyms, health food stores, laundries, and coffee shops. Printing cards with the meeting times and locations for members to give to any interested person, a sign at the meeting locations while we are there, and fliers on the bulletin boards when we are not, offer additional opportunities for name recognition and carrying the message.

This is the beginning. Continuing to get reporters interested in our Society is also possible with local information added for publication in our areas. Other methods include having bookmarks with information about GSA at the local libraries and available on our GreySheet.org site and encouraging the Public Information Committee to invite sharing of samples of what local groups have produced so that others might generate theirs, while the Public Information Committee gets materials approved by the World Service Conference.

So what is "the group's message"? Ours is one of hope and faith and JOY. Our local groups are active and encourage participation and service within the group and with visiting GSAs. When someone is hospitalized locally or is considering GreySheeters Anonymous as an alternative, we reach out. We had helped several become more conscious of their eating habits even when GSA did not seem to them the right solution. We have planted seeds for potential growth.

We have faith that what we are attempting to do will bring results for ourselves and others, even if not GSA. We continue to strive to carry the GSA message. Those who have been abstinent longer share how they carry the message of hope and recovery with others. Seed planting and more seed planting one day at a time and one person at a time are methods to share. Letting people know what we do and sharing about our individual recoveries are additional means to share about GreySheeters Anonymous and how it works.

Primary Purpose

Recently, our group has needed to review Tradition Five. Our group's primary purpose is to carry its message to the compulsive eater who still suffers. Are we doing that effectively? It was the topic of many business meetings. We talked about ways to reach out to the community. We left business cards and pamphlets on bulletin boards, on tables in Employee Assistance Programs, at work, in churches, and in doctors' offices.

I attended the first WSC, and I was amazed that GSA groups were getting bigger and bigger all over the world, and in my town where our mantra started, GSA groups were getting smaller. How could this be? Was it because so many GreySheeters had double-digit back to back abstinence and had become complacent with meeting attendance? Was it because phone meetings were available, and people didn't want to leave the house? I brought the facts back from the WSC and told the area groups about growth in other locales. One area group decided to hold an Information Session. Posters were put up in our area. Announcements were placed in the newspaper. Emails were sent to Health Services of area universities. We all decided that it was time to spread the word. If people were struggling with food, GSA might be an option for them.

I respect all members' anonymity. I understand everyone has a different comfort level with disclosure of food addiction. I eat my breakfast and lunch in a public setting. I work in an environment where people show gratitude with large boxes of foods we avoid. It never takes long for my colleagues to notice that I don't eat the way they do. I am quick to tell them that I lost 100 pounds 20 years ago and follow a program that ensures that I keep it off. They are typically shocked and refuse to believe it's true. I show them "before" pictures that are on my phone, and they are amazed. They come to me and "confess" what they have eaten. They ask me if they should have "x" or "y." I tell them I don't know. I weigh and measure my food from the GreySheet three times a day, give it to my sponsor, and don't eat in between my meals. I never know when a person may be willing to do what we do. It's a program of attraction, not promotion.

It is important to me to see a cohesive, thriving GreySheet community in my town and all over the world! Helping another person struggling with food is what my soul needs to do. It fortifies my abstinence. I have to give back what was so freely given to me. No Matter What.

Service

This Tradition Five is one of the reasons that keeps me going to my very small group when I know that I might be the only person there that night. There have been a few times when I showed up, and I was the only one. And conversely, there were times when I sat there, with my books and writing in hand, spending the hour sometimes listening to a CD from a GreySheet Roundup. Sometimes my thinking will start along the lines, "This is ridiculous. Coming here tired from work, wanting to go home, having to drive another hour after this so-called meeting, before I can get home from my long day." Dear Reader, you can see how my thinking degenerates, but every once in a while, when I am the only one at a meeting, someone comes in (invariably late,) but a visitor is looking for a GreySheeters Anonymous meeting, because at that moment in life, she is suffering and thinks about getting abstinent. It is at those times that I feel the grace of God working in my life, because I can speak about our disease with this person who might have left discouraged if I had not been there. I remember a few of these occasions, and this keeps me going.

This winter there have been many snow and ice storms, and I have not felt able to drive to our meeting. My vision is getting worse now in the dark, and our roads are icy and full of potholes. My courage just isn't there to drive 45 minutes after work and then to drive another hour home after the meeting. But there is another person who does make it many times when I cannot. She and I have both shared about these times when we are the only ones at the meeting and about how important it is that someone be there, to carry the message.

Tradition Five Questions:

1. What is the primary purpose of each GSA group?
2. How does a group 'carry its message?' What is the process?
3. What is 'its message?'
4. How does this process serve the individual and the group? What are the outcomes? Inside and outside GSA?
5. How can I become more focused in carrying the message?
6. Who is the 'compulsive eater who still suffers?'
7. What specific methods can we use to carry the message?
8. What keeps me from carrying the message?
9. How can this group carry the message to those who still suffer from compulsive eating?
10. Who will take the next steps to put into reality each of these specific ideas?

Tradition Six: A GSA group ought never endorse, finance, or lend the GSA name to any related facility or outside enterprise, lest problems of money, property, and prestige divert us from our primary purpose.

The Sixth Tradition seeks to avoid any complications with products, organizations, companies, and institutions for fear that entanglements could interfere with successfully addressing our primary purpose, which is to stay abstinent and to carry the message to other compulsive eaters who still suffer.

Tradition Six reminds the group to avoid lending the GSA name to any enterprise or event 'outside' GSA, no matter how appropriate the cause might seem to be. We cannot lend our name to any rehabilitation centers, eating disorder clinics, or counseling groups. GSA could not handle associations with these other entities. They may have a profit motive or sink into political or ethical difficulties. GSA remains separate instead.

To attach our GSA name to other Twelve Step programs serves neither organization. Each Twelve Step program stands on its own without associations that may create more dependency and hazards than the potential benefits. By definition, we are not aligned with any other organization.

The official GSA website, www.greysheet.org, does not suggest particular brands, stores, or Internet sites where members might purchase items and foods we use in abstinence. In accord with our Sixth Tradition, we do not want to create even the appearance of association or alignment with other organizations. For instance, if a source for a certain electronic scale or a particular brand of food product were posted on our website, it might appear as an endorsement. Individually, we freely share our experience about particular brands of appliances or food, but as a fellowship we abstain from any 'official' alliances.

We once posted lists of free resources, suggestions for legal assistance, or other Twelve Step program resources on our website. At first, we believed these connections supported us and would help our members, but the wisdom of the Sixth Tradition emerged, and we realized that posting information about other organizations would require vetting, maintaining, and updating this information on our website. This would take time and effort that could be used to carry the GSA message of recovery. We cannot sell scales or legal aid. We need to concentrate on our purpose of staying abstinent and helping those who still suffer.

We do put links on our website for information about GSA meetings and events. There is also information online for newcomers about how to find a GSA sponsor and get started. There is information about GS groups intergroups, and world services and how members can contribute to support GSA. We are confident that any information about outside issues and sources that individuals, groups, or intergroups need can be located through shared experience, strength, and hope. Information more directly pertinent to our GSA program is also available from our pamphlets, service manuals, and other GSA guidelines.

We take this adherence to GSA tenets to heart in our meetings, too. When outside issues are raised at meetings, such as political, religious, or other debates, we have learned to keep our eyes on our plates. We do not discuss other programs, and we abstain from touting our individual beliefs, whether religious, political, financial, or any other.

What do we do about a member who perhaps is a celebrity; however, this person goes between circuit speaking and being drunk on the food and 'out there' because he or she cannot tolerate or enjoy the notoriety or anonymity? We as GSA members offer the love and respect offered to any newcomer. We offer a program that works for those who work it. We offer abstinence and clarity of mind. We offer freedom from compulsive eating and food addiction.

The resources we share do include money in the seventh tradition; however, if money were the only resource, we would all be diminished. The joy we share with others may help each of us. The shared experience, strength, and hope help us to carry our message into the world.

The central fact for each of us is that GSA is one compulsive eater sharing with another. One day at a time we have a reprieve from this progressive and potentially lethal disease with a program based on a spiritual solution. How much money one has or does not have is a non-issue in GSA.

To align ourselves with others, even the very worthy causes, groups, resources, and companies, which some have requested, might lead to the demise of GSA. To continue to carry the message to another compulsive eater who still suffers, we use our personal resources of time, energy, enthusiasm, and money. We also support our intergroups with similar resources to reach out even further into the world of compulsive eaters and food addicts who still suffer and whom we may never meet face-to-face.

When anyone, anywhere reaches out for help, let GSA always be there. We might say, "I am one messenger of hope to another compulsive eater who still suffers. For that, I am responsible. Let it begin with me."

Tradition Six Personal Experiences:

Singleness of Purpose

Numerous examples in our GSA history have brought to the forefront the necessity of this Tradition. One of our discussion meetings included the topic of what constitutes a GreySheeters Anonymous meeting or group? The singleness of purpose plays a part here as we focus on GreySheeters Anonymous recovery to support GSA with our time, money, energy, and service.

If we are connecting our GSA program with other 12 Step programs instead of staying focused on our single shared purpose, we may lose the gift that we have to offer others in the world. Mixing and matching can be done in one on one sharing as perceived needed at the moment. In the groups and in our meetings the abstinence from endorsing or financing or lending the GSA name to any outside enterprises does work.

When the problems of "money, property, and prestige divert us from our primary purpose" we lose the gift, the joy of service, and the hope of recovery and unity which allow us to continue to grow individually and collectively in our fellowship.

For me, I need to remember that my abstinent recovery is the most important thing in my life today. I cannot attach the GreySheeters Anonymous name to any outside enterprise, no matter how worthy a cause it may be. What had started out so successfully in another organization, met its demise because it lost its singleness of purpose and primary aim.

Let us not suffer the same fate. Let us choose clarity of mind and focus: our single primary purpose is to carry the message of recovery to those who still suffer from compulsive eating. Let nothing stand in the way of this hope and focus.

Stick to What We Know

Tradition Six ensures that GSA will not be teaming up with any other programs. We stick to what we know. Our primary purpose is to stay abstinent and help others to recover from compulsive eating. We don't have to worry about financial issues, real estate, or where we fall on the top 40 popular food programs. These don't matter. We are people who suffered terribly with food and have found a common solution. Our solution works for anyone who is WILLING to work it. It is a program that addresses a three-fold disease: spiritual, mental, and physical. I carry the message to all who suffer. It doesn't matter where they live, if they work, if they have a family, or if they are the same political party. Tradition Six keeps it one compulsive eater/food addict sharing with another compulsive eater/food addict.

Paid in Full

I went to a commercial weight loss program once for a few months. It was created to make money, as any business is. Products to buy were everywhere and were placed on a table before you even signed up for a session. I can imagine products would be handy for us at meetings, for instance, scales and other measuring equipment, certain foods, and sweeteners, but how sticky all of this could get. Who would do the ordering? Would we have salespeople coming to meetings? Would some people be enticed to become spokespersons, maybe even on television or in print? My egotistically-inclined imagination could start numerous scenarios.

The traditions keep me humble. I have been given a gift that I can keep if I give it away. I do not sell it. There is no other reason for me to be at a meeting than to keep my abstinence and to help others with theirs. I do not ask to be paid for my service work, because I know that it is helping me and will possibly help someone like me who was stuck in the terrible struggle of compulsive eating: ashamed, horrified, in denial, and getting sicker.

We see advertising everywhere. It is a relief to go to meetings and not have pop-up ads, banners of companies, or endorsed products. I don't have to wonder where the money goes. I know where it goes, and it too has a spiritual directive, which is to help the still-suffering compulsive eater.

At the meetings, it is important to concentrate on the GreySheeters Anonymous message: how to abstain from compulsive eating with the help of GSA and how to stay abstinent one day at a time no matter what.

Tradition Six Questions:

1. What does it mean to 'lend' the GSA name? In what circumstances has the opportunity arisen and been refused?
2. Give examples of erring on the side of accumulation. (Cluttering/hoarding may be a common experience of many members.)
3. Give examples of erring on the side of dispersal. (To debt in time or money may be a common experience of many members.)
4. Why abstain from giving specific advice instead of general guidelines to GreySheet communities? What is the advantage of the general guidelines shared in our worldwide community?
5. How can we apply Tradition Six in our families and work relationships? In other social relationships?
6. Why pay professionals when we could have so many volunteers? Consider the availability and the means to provide continuity of services 24 hours a day around the world.
7. How does one create a personal sense of balance regarding money, property or prestige? How does one with another create the interpersonal sense of balance regarding money, property or prestige?
8. How does the separation of the spiritual and financial help and/or hinder GSA?
9. Ultimately, how might our decisions about money, property, and prestige affect our ability to carry the GSA message to the still-suffering compulsive eater?

Tradition Seven: Every GSA group ought to be fully self-supporting, declining outside contributions.

Self-supporting compulsive eaters; do they exist? How many of us, addicts to the core, spent excessively while bingeing, unconcerned about those around us? How many others pinched every penny, except for the money spent on our substances? Many of us were dependent on a spouse, a parent, a partner, or a series of friends for financial support. Some had been independent, yet searched hungrily for someone on whom to be dependent or for someone who would "take care" of things. In money matters, we may have been selfish and unreliable. Experience with GreySheet abstinence and the GSA program gave us a new set of priorities. Some of the funds that once allowed us to eat compulsively now contribute to support healthy GS recovery and GSA.

The only requirement for GSA membership is a desire to stop eating compulsively, and only individuals who are members may contribute to GSA. There are no dues or fees for membership, but as each member gains and maintains abstinence, works the steps, and learns the importance of Tradition Seven to support our primary purpose, each learns that giving financial support to the organization is part of the recovery process.

We do not seek grants or accept financial donations from non-members. While some who have interests in treatment facilities for compulsive eaters, new diet foods, or other non-GSA solutions offer financial support, their money cannot be accepted because it would come with "strings attached." Our focus is continuous abstinence and helping the compulsive eaters who still suffer. Only GSA members and those Board Members who are not GSA members share their expertise and can be involved in the determination of GSA money matters.

As in each household, financial support is not the only form of support needed. Groups need volunteers at meeting sites to open the door for a newcomer or a visitor who needs a meeting. GSA needs members willing to accept the responsibility to get a newcomer started with our food plan or to be a food or service sponsor. Money is not the essence of GSA. Our shared experience, strength, and hope serve as our main currency. Passing on what we have learned and how we learned it shows that we individually and collectively can make a difference using our time, energy, and enthusiasm. The services rendered by member-volunteers to support the group, intergroup, and world services are essential. Volunteers serve as bookers, speakers, leaders, treasurers, internet participants, moderators, web servants, World Service Board members, Conference Committee members, sponsors, and leaders of A Way of Life groups. The largest number of volunteers are speakers and sponsors, sharing their experience, strength, and hope. This sharing and each of the other volunteer jobs help support recovery and our primary purpose. We need to carry the message to individuals, institutions, and other public entities. The Public Information Committee, for example, works to ensure that GreySheeters Anonymous has name recognition in the public to better serve our purpose.

Arguing about money and how it should or should not be spent at the group or intergroup business meeting does happen. However, whether the resources should be conserved or expended. Whatever the volume of the discussion, we do usually come to a point at which we agree to disagree until we have a group conscience. We are self-supporting through our contributions and need to support our groups, intergroups, and GSAWS. We do encourage each other to focus on the spiritual paths we walk. Without financial resources at the group, intergroup, and world services levels, literature, public information and general upkeep for our fellowship will be impacted.

We need places to meet and share one-on-one and with a group. We need professionals to maintain the website and GSA administrative responsibilities that for years were carried by volunteers. When the hours require a change from a few hours a week to a half or full time job, then we need to pay an appropriate wage for these services. We need to have a service structure and committees that create public information documents, radio spots, and publish literature to carry the unique message of GSA. For this, we may need to hire professional editors, writers, and designers. We need the skills of a parliamentarian and transcriber to aid us in our World

Service Conferences. We continue to welcome and benefit from members' volunteer service; however, when these jobs become too time-consuming, they eventually negatively affect the individual and the organization. We then need to hire professionals who may or may not be GSA members.

More than one group wondered why the donation checks to GSAWS were cashed so slowly and why the only response they received was a cancelled check, delayed for months with no 'receipt' or recognition for the donations sent. At that time, volunteers were picking up the mail from the post office box 'every month or so,' sorting it, and then sending it on to other volunteers in other parts of the city or country to record its receipt, before it was finally deposited. These practices did not demonstrate sound fiscal management to the GSA constituency.

As intergroups formed, small offices and telephone services were established, and some achieved non-profit status. The GSAWS Board of Trustees acknowledged the need for administrative support, website technical support, professional publishing support. Volunteers could not do it all, and the technology required to serve meeting groups and provide information over the Internet was not free.

We require at times the talents of an accountant or attorney for matters relating to our incorporation and non-profit standing.

We are responsible for serving our entire fellowship's inverted triangle with the funds we collect, from the groups down through their GSRs to the intergroups, and through their Intergroup Service Representatives to the World Service Conference and Board of Trustees. Board members and other delegates regularly meet for World Service Conferences. The groups support the intergroups and GSAWS. The intergroups support GSAWS; therefore all our delegates can attend WSC supported by groups and intergroups.

Our money matters have not always been easy. Disagreements about how money should be spent have come up at group and intergroup business meetings. Sometimes we reached a point where we agreed to disagree until we could schedule a group conscience. Then we voted, heard the minority opinion, and moved on to another topic. A new (second) vote could be requested if a member who voted in the majority acknowledged a change of heart after hearing the minority opinion. That one person's change of vote is enough to trigger a revote. The outcome of this second vote stands. Sometimes, we have "gone to the hat," a 12 Step means to resolve an especially thorny issue.

Balance is a necessary addition. For those who 'people please,' acceptance of too many roles in service may overwhelm. It was not unheard of for a member overextended in service to collect enough resentments to eat again. This served no one except those who observed and learned the lesson second hand. Individuals learned that balance was crucial. Weighing and measuring our food, selected from the GreySheet, not eating between meals no matter what, working with a sponsor, service in GSA, meeting attendance, and work on the steps and traditions, all ground us individually to maintain abstinence. Abstinence expands to include abstinence from power plays, abstinence from unduly influencing others, abstinence from self-pity and resentments, and abstinence from over- or underworking. Following the GS food plan, the way we do in GSA, serves as the basis for growth and change in other areas through the step, tradition, and concept work.

The groups support the General Service Representatives' (GSRs') participation in the next level down on the inverted triangle. The intergroups support the Intergroup Service Representatives' (ISRs') participation in the next level down on the inverted triangle. Groups and intergroups support GreySheeters Anonymous World Services (GSAWS.) GSAWS supports the Board of Trustees in their participation in the World Service Conference. Each group supports its representatives financially and with information and the 'right of decision' in the concepts.

The rent and other costs in the group are paid, and a prudent reserve is set aside. The groups and intergroups monthly send donations to their intergroups and directly to World Service. The prudent reserve may include funds for a monthly disbursement by the group and intergroup if needed. Intergroups pay their expenses, maintain a prudent reserve, and also send the rest as a donation to GSAWS. In this way, GSAWS can provide services that benefit the whole fellowship. The support of the Intergroup and GSAWS is not from our excess but our continuous abundance. We are self- supporting.

'Self-supporting' relates to the financial support for all levels of the GSA inverted triangle and originates from contributions from individual GSA members. As the first GSA World Service Conference approached, questions arose about paying for the expenses of the members who would serve as GSA delegates. Ideally, all delegates would be fully-funded. The level (group, intergroup, or World Service) would pay for all of the travel, lodging, and food expenses for their respective voting delegates and an additional sum to cover conference expenses, including the parliamentarian, transcribers, meeting rooms, and equipment.

GSAWS cannot be swayed from our primary purpose. GSAWS' running expenses and a prudent reserve are essential, but wealth and lavish accommodations do not fit our primary purpose. As an organization, we encourage our groups, intergroups, and World Services to be self-supporting through our contributions. We need to focus on regularly sharing with the GSA groups that their donations are received and what those funds support. The treasurer's reports on GreySheet.org offer this information monthly. Intergroups report to their constituencies, just as trusted servants report to their individual groups.

The importance of being self-supporting through our contributions as individuals is also a goal post, as members of families and groups, and as GSA as a whole. We are learning to care for ourselves with weighed and measured food and then with our work, service, and bank accounts.

Individuals, groups, and intergroups support their own groups, intergroups, and GSAWS in order to carry the message of recovery to those who still suffer from this progressive and potentially fatal disease of compulsive eating/food addiction.

Participation in service at all levels presses each member to grow into new responsibilities personally and publicly. Service shared freely enhances each person's program and aids in the development of skills and self-esteem.

We are self-supporting through our contributions, but we do not focus on money. We encourage each other to focus on abstinence and the spiritual paths we walk to carry the message to other compulsive eaters. This is a place where money is needed, but it is not the central focus. What do I put in the face-to-face meeting baskets in other 12 step groups? The answer might serve as a model for appropriate GSA giving. Many 12 step programs encourage multiple dollar donations daily when members can donate.

If a GreySheet member does not have funds with which to contribute, other contributions are valid too. The member need only stay. The day comes when funds are more readily available. Contributions can wait until a member is no longer debting to recognize the importance of the basket.

Tradition Seven Personal Experiences:

Self-Supporting

Every GSA group ought to be self-supporting in all ways, supporting itself financially and fully supported with available trusted servants to serve in all the positions needed to have a fully functioning group. Additionally, the group members handle paying the expenses of their trusted servants to be certain that any competent member might serve without impacting his or her personal or familial finances. Last but not least, the Group gives support to both the Intergroup and GSAWS.

Declining outside contributions might mean declining offers of cash from a group outside the fellowship; no matter how well-meaning the gift might be, gifts from non-GSA members are not accepted. When we visit a group, contributions are appropriate. Would our contributions to a group other than our home group be considered an outside proposition? We are part of the same fellowship and may donate as we wish when it is given with no strings attached.

With the fellowship as a whole, then the self-support might include all members, as in a request to the members of the fellowship to celebrate the anniversary of GSAWS with fundraisers within GSA to generate sufficient funds. Then no one would pay more than his or her share.

What is the purpose of a prudent reserve? The traditional answer is to have money sufficient for one or more months of rent, beverages, and the contributions to the Intergroup and GSAWS in case the meetings have a downturn in funds. Are there other reasons to use the prudent reserve? Might the prudent reserve be used to send a delegate to the GSA World Service Conference? This too is a reasonable use of money that has been collected by the group. The prudent reserve might be refilled subsequently with group members' donations. A separate account for collecting funds for delegates is sometimes chosen.

After due consideration, there are expenses for a group in addition to paying the rent. If the rent is so high that the rent is barely made with repeated passes of the donation basket, does self-supporting suggest the end of meetings in that particular location? Perhaps the meeting needs a different meeting place to invite more participation in the entire program.

Action in GSA is important. Generosity and abundance demonstrated in the financial arena of groups, intergroups, and GSAWS are also ways in which we can assist new and old groups alike.

Concerning our families - when we are self-supporting financially, emotionally, and spiritually, we are grateful and experience abundance. Self-support may mean different things over the course of a lifetime as individuals in different couples make choices about how they will spend their money in diverse ways. It is each family's right to decide that education is necessary to promote success. Self-supporting, in my household, means that I live within my means and save for items I want or need. It means that I am honest with my income. I abstain from secrets regarding funds.

Sponsoring sponsees through the steps and then the traditions and concepts and offering to be a service sponsor to aid trusted servants and future trustees do their jobs more successfully are service sponsor examples. These are gifts of time and energy.

GSA meetings are self-supporting through the group members' contributions. This makes it the responsibility of the members to pay the rent, fund a prudent reserve, contribute to the Intergroup resources, send a percentage to World Service, and maintain a supply of literature (including GreySheet food plans paid through the intergroup to which the group belongs.) Additional literature, when available, will be my choice to purchase and use. I look forward to using GreySheeters Anonymous literature as another way to support our program.

Doing My Share

Supporting GSA is not only a financial contribution. I attend my meetings and make myself available to newcomers. I attend the business meeting monthly and take an active role. I volunteer for service positions. I serve in the local Intergroup. I am on the Communications Committee for World Service. This program saved my life; my service is a small price to pay. I cannot rest on my laurels thinking that "someone else will do service," because what if they do not? I share with my sponsees and my group the importance of doing service. Serving the group, the Intergroup, and GSA as a whole is the responsibility of each member. That responsibility is much more manageable when it's carried by many.

Accepting my annual medallion during the group meeting is important to me, as it shows that the program works if I work it. It shows newcomers that it is possible to put together years, and even decades of back to back abstinence. I look forward to newcomers gaining abstinence and being able to accept service positions. I will gladly pass the torch when the time comes.

Tradition Seven Questions:

1. What does self-supporting through our contributions mean personally, in a workplace, in a group, and in GSA as a whole?
2. In what ways do I support myself? My family? My group? GSAWS?
3. What more can I do now to increase support for my GSA group, my family, and GSAWS with my finances, time, and commitment?
4. Do I send a personal contribution to GSAWS in celebration of my yearly anniversary of abstinence and my belly button birthday? A monthly contribution? An annual birthday gift in April for GSAWS?
5. Does my group pay for rent, beverages, and literature? For Intergroup and GSAWS donations?
6. What methods have I used, other than financial, to support the group?
7. Do I attend and support business meetings and group conscience for my group? Do I ask for business meetings to be regularly scheduled?
8. What has been the outcome for me personally as a result of what I do? What do I receive personally for my service to GSA?
9. How often and regularly are service positions rotated in my group or intergroup? In GSAWS?
10. How can I encourage others to give service?
11. How can I increase my service to GSAWS?
12. How does my group support in non-monetary ways our intergroup? GSAWS?
13. How can I carry the message to those who have limited phone service and funds?
14. Do I share my positive GSA pitches regularly at meetings, in writing on Internet sites, or send my qualification to the website? Or audio sites? If not, shall I?
15. Does my group have a treasurer who gives reports regularly?
16. How do I evaluate my self-worth? Money? How much am I needed by others? Do I give humble anonymous service?
17. Do I fear to release the responsibilities for leadership to newer members? Do they fear to accept the responsibilities? How might I support the newer members to do the tasks as they gain confidence?

18. How can I learn to stand independently and interdependently and allow others to do the same for all to gain self-respect?
19. Am I self-supporting? If not, how might I redress the situation? Am I underemployed? Am I under-earning?
20. Do I accept and share my feelings without explanation or denial?
21. Am I responsible for my feelings or do I point the blame finger? How can I mature?
22. Am I dependent on the weather, the body scale, or another person for my sense of well-being? If so, what might I do to redress this imbalance?
23. Do I express gratitude to all those who encourage my abstinence and continued growth and maturation?
24. In what other ways can my groups and I be more self-supporting through our contributions?
25. Do my groups regularly donate to the Intergroup and GSAWS? If not, why not? What can I do to ensure fulfillment of our primary purpose?
26. How does the separation of spiritual and financial matters help and hinder GSA?

Tradition Eight: GreySheeters Anonymous should remain forever nonprofessional, but our service centers may employ special workers.

Tradition Eight guides us to accept that we are all non-professionals as we share our individual experience, strength, and hope with other compulsive eaters. Each member of GSA had life experiences prior to coming to the program and even more experiences since coming to the program. Those of us who benefited from what was freely given to us, pass on what we were given and what happened as a result. When a newcomer hears a fellow compulsive eater share his/her story and can identify, one compulsive eater with another, comfort and direction are expressed in a way that is different from any other relationship. There is relief in knowing that there are other people with the same unmanageable disease who have found a solution.

The Twelve Step programs, and specifically GSA, allow and encourage this 'no cost' sharing of experience, strength, and hope. The process benefits both the speaker and the listener. Each of us grows as we share or pass on what we learned from another GSA member. All too often, the topic we share with a newcomer is just what we need to hear. We sometimes need a reminder to begin to practice some aspect of the program again that we have been neglecting. Recovery through service is one of our tools and has repeatedly been demonstrated to help the one who shares as much, and sometimes more, than the recipient.

A positive attitude and frequent repeating of what works support continued abstinence for those who serve by sharing, in our meeting rooms and on our phone meetings, one compulsive eater shares with another. There are many professionals in GSA who are recovering from compulsive eating and food addictions. When they speak, however, they share their humble experience, strength, and hope in recovery in our program.

Some GSA areas opened service centers staffed by volunteers. When the telephone, literature, and public information needs in an area grow and outstrip the freely-given service hours available from the fellowship, the area may employ special workers with the skills needed to perform the work. The appropriate pay for these skill sets is the proper pay scale for the skills in the area. Even if the special worker is a 'two hatter,' a member of our program and a current employee of the program, he or she deserves a reasonable wage.

Tradition Eight reminds us to carry the message of recovery to others. Special workers help us accomplish the clerical work by maintaining regular hours to answer the telephones and respond to emails in a timely fashion. Unlike a member-volunteer, special workers do not carry our message, but their work allows member-volunteers and their hours to support GSA conferences, meetings, intergroups, the phone meetings, the internet service, and world service. The combined efforts of paid special workers and members sharing their experience, strength, and hope with another suffering compulsive eater make possible the growth of our program and its expansion to serve the needs of more who suffer from compulsive eating and food addiction.

Tradition Eight Personal Experiences:

How We Spend Funds on Service

When I first found GSA, I wanted to share my ESH with everyone all the time. I was so excited to have found the easier, softer way! I couldn't believe that after all of the weight loss gimmicks and programs I had tried and all of the money I had wasted, my Higher Power had guided me to a program that was FREE and for the first time in my life I was free from cravings. It was a miracle. It still is a miracle. I had a tendency to 'preach' instead of share. I had a lack of humility. I learned that what other people do with food is not my business, and it is not my job to become a spokesperson. Today, I humbly share my experience, strength, and hope with folks who ask what I'm doing with my food. I like to remember that GSA is a program of attraction, not promotion.

GSA has remained non-professional but employs special workers. We have hired someone to help build and maintain our website; we hired a parliamentarian to help guide us in our WSC. A transcriber documented all of our voting sessions during the first WSC. We have hired lawyers and accountants. I am grateful to all of the groups for helping support GSA projects.

I give service on a local and worldwide level. It has enriched my abstinence and my life. It is refreshing to make connections all over the world. It is inspiring to hear my fellow travelers say the GreySheet mantra – I weigh and measure my food three times a day from the GreySheet, write it down, and call it into a sponsor. I don't eat no matter what!!

Special Workers: Yes

In my experience, it is essential that our organization employ special workers when there is a need, and it has enough money to do so. Some competent people in service positions become overwhelmed and sooner or later get burned out. Many lack 12 Step service experience at the levels beyond the group. The traditions demand skills that develop over time. Time takes time. We are food addicts in recovery. At times, we are in service positions requiring different levels of skills, commitment, and responsibility than many GSAs possess when we arrive in GSA and may not be prepared to give. Some initially gave substantial service; however, rotation of service is essential. When we employ workers for administrative tasks, members can pass on the message of hope.

The beauty of twelfth step work and that which gives us the ability to touch others in a deeper way than a professional is that we have the experience of being a compulsive eater, and for myself, a sugar addict. I can freely talk about my addiction and my allergy to foods that cause the phenomenon of craving and keep me in bondage. I am proud of my slim figure, but I know deep down, that I could not have done this alone, that the program was given to me by another compulsive eater, and I was ready to accept the gift at that moment. I had not heard the message for a number of years even after I had been introduced to it.

Tradition Eight Questions:

1. Do I willingly share my experience, strength, and hope (ESH) with others?
2. Do I ever sound like a professional instead of sharing my ESH?
3. Do I give service regularly? Do I give enough to feel the benefits of the self-esteem that come from giving service?
4. When I am into my self-pity, do I reach out to listen to others? What do I use as a spiritual guide for my daily life?
5. How can I employ this tradition in my home, with my partner, at work?
6. Am I willing to help pay for workers who are employed as agents of GSA?
7. Where is the line between sharing ESH and giving too much?
8. Do I trust that each of us can choose to live a happy, joyous, and free life?

Tradition Nine: GSA, as such, ought never be organized; but we may create service boards or committees directly responsible to those they serve.

Twelve Step organizations have no membership rules or requirements, except for the desire to be abstinent from the substances or behaviors that used to harm us. We have no local governing bodies. We have no elected officials. We are a loosely woven fabric that is substantial, nevertheless. No one can tell another member what to do or what not to do. We simply share our experience, strength, and hope with each other.

Our program, like those 12 step programs before us, created service boards or committees to serve the organization. These bodies are directly responsible to the membership they serve (groups, intergroups, committees, WSC, and the Board of Trustees.)

A Board of Trustees served as corporate officers (required for incorporation) until the World Service Conference Committee formed and organized the first World Service Conference (WSC) in Philadelphia in 2013. The WSC standing committees include:

1. The Public Information Committee (PIC), acts as a liaison between GSA and the general population. The Committee's goal is to increase awareness of the GSA program using GSA Conference Approved Literature, posters, and the GSA website. The Committee serves as a resource for newcomers. Professional web and layout designers and editors may work with this committee.
2. The Literature Committee (LC), assures that every aspect of the GSA program of recovery is presented in a comprehensive and consistent written form. Literature includes books, pamphlets, leaflets, and other material that is reviewed and approved for

distribution to our members, friends, professionals, and to the world at large via the GSA website and other locales.

3. The Structure Committee (SC) makes recommendations for the GSA service structure. The Structure Manual includes board policies, guidelines, procedures, job descriptions, and standard practices that have been approved by the WSC. The Structure Committee also looks at the bylaws and Conference Charter and proposes changes. It may serve as a Nomination Committee, and members may do the footwork to assist the Board Nominating Committee develop the slate of Trustees and Officers who are officially voted in at WSC.
4. The Finance Committee (FC) provides stewardship over the procedures by which the funds received by GSAWS are used. It develops and implements guidelines and procedures in all matters concerning the finances of GSA, including ways and means to generate funds necessary for the continued growth of the fellowship and the transparent reporting of GSAWS finances to the fellowship. The anniversary gifts on individual's birthdays or anniversaries and on the anniversary of our April 6, 1998, founding of GSA are examples. Monthly committed donations from a credit/debit card or bank account are additional means for individuals and groups to support GSAWS.
5. The Communications Committee (CC) develops guidelines for the use of the communication-related technology such as web pages, internet groups, and others like "Service Matters."
6. The Logistics (LOG) or Conference Committee handles all aspects of the annual GSA World Service Conference. Its purpose is to organize the WSC for the coming year, which includes selecting possible dates and places. The delegates vote at each conference for a subsequent WSC. The LOG prepares the WSC agenda, selects a parliamentarian and transcriber, requests funding from GSAWS or paid from conference funds, prepares registration packets, and oversees the logistics of each WSC including the placement of delegates in working committees.
7. The Legal Committee handles protection of our copyright of the GreySheet food plan, the trademark, and literature. It is also responsible for addressing non-profit status, indemnification of the Board members and any other legal issues brought to it.

8. The Archives Committee handles developing appropriate storage and maintenance of historical documents in GSA history, literature, and paperwork that documents the legal and historical aspects of GSAWS, the intergroups, and Groups.

Besides these committees, additional committees can be formed, as they are needed.

Legal issues regarding the grey piece of paper that we all hold as the basis of our abstinence were first met with attempts to avoid the issues at hand. The fact remained; we did not own the copyright for the food plan for which our program was named. Were we to be a legal and ethical organization or not? It was a difficult time as many were inclined to continue to fight instead of acknowledge copyright law and move on to what we could do. The attachment of many to a single two-sided piece of paper that had changed our lives and had in practice changed over the years was the sticking point. Some wanted to change the written portions to match what many do.

We shared disagreement about so many particulars that the only thing we shared universally was the grey. Some communities spoke in their format of following the program of another twelve-step program and used 'powerless over alcohol' even after the GSAWS Board of Trustees had adopted the Twelve Steps of our new program using the word "food."

We are 'powerless over food' because some members are compulsive overeaters, some bulimics, and some anorexics. Some are food addicts or volume eaters are as sensitive to grains, sugars, oils, or carbohydrates. The differences are vast.

The resolution finally came with an external source saying 'cease and desist' distributing the GreySheet. Legal and financial solutions followed. Now as the owner of the GreySheet food plan, we have a responsibility to protect our copyright and GSAWS has the right to copy and distribute the GreySheet. This initially was done with stipulations, and then permission granted to some intergroups. This process changed to one in which GreySheets are sold to intergroups at a nominal cost. Intergroups provide them to GSRs and GSRs provide them to sponsors for their sponsees. In this way, the GreySheet comes with a sponsor. Over the years, the small cost for each GreySheet will recoup the legal and purchase costs in addition to the printer's charges to return the GreySheet to its 1972 "look and feel" while deleting the previous owner's name and adding the required permission to use the steps.

An adolescent organization is saving lives. Abstinence is gained while the resolutions are in the making. Without directives, without punishments other than those that are natural consequences of actions taken, and without any means to banish members, the organization continues to develop and grow.

Individuals share their experience, strength, and hope. Groups pass on their collective experience, strength, and hope. Only suggestions or mildly phrased referrals to our literature are in fact given to those who inquire at GSAWS or greysheet.org.

Issues that arose in the past included concerns about the resources on the website: recipes, suggested means to obtain foods and scales, the distribution of the GreySheet, and the formats for meetings. Other concerns that arose were the issues regarding the part that the previous literature would play in the new program. Concerns expressed focus on our primary purpose and different views of how best to transmit our solution for compulsive eating and food addiction.

Even with the mild manner in which responses, if any, were posed, the spiritual outcomes that would occur as a result of disobedience to the steps, traditions, and concepts were outcomes that were natural consequences of disregard. The disease is both physical and spiritual in nature. Consequences of disobedience to the principles of our program are both physical and spiritual. Loss of abstinence, despair, and sooner or later, death may result from such disobedience.

Individuals and groups alike conform to the Steps & Traditions or suffer the consequences. Thus, we submit to the principles because we love the physical, intellectual, emotional, and spiritual lives that we have. The disciplinarians of all the Twelve Step program folks remain love and suffering. No others have been needed.

The service boards and committees are essential to complete the tasks of GSA. Each group elects the members who serve locally and who go to Intergroup. Then comes the formation of intergroups and the election or selection by the "going to the hat" method for members to be delegates to the World Service Conference. There is no authority in particular persons. The Board of Trustees for GSAWS is responsible to the GSA Fellowship as a whole through the World Service Conference delegates, up through the intergroups to the groups at the top of the inverted triangle.

Thus, as the personal goal of each member is abstinence, the goal of our service is to bring the opportunity to attain and maintain abstinence to anyone who suffers. If individual members were unwilling to serve and share experience, strength, and hope, the needs of others might not be met, and all of us would suffer the consequences. The spirit of service is what keeps our need for the program fresh. Without keeping it green, we might all suffer the consequences. Instead, we remain GreySheet abstinent and share with others through service the gifts of abstinence and how to attain and maintain abstinence.

GSA is a growing program that has survived its infancy and has come into adolescence by adhering to the principles of the Twelve Steps & Twelve Traditions. We are all equal in this democratic organization and are striving to stay abstinent and share the message of recovery with those who still suffer. Service is the key.

Tradition Nine Personal Experiences:

Chaos or Organization

Several circumstances have brought to the front aspects of this tradition. When is it okay to have a committee or a service board? What is an organization? What is chaos? How might we be organized enough to support our primary purpose without being so disorganized that we limit the group and its autonomy, except when it affects other groups or GSA as a whole? These issues have come up and continue to arise.

One example is the organization of intergroups. At one period, we were meeting weekly or twice weekly to discuss how the GSA organization might be structured. In this period, the intergroups were discussed at length. It was determined that intergroups could be a time slot or day on the phone bridge or a geographic locale including three to eight meetings or groups. GreySheeters Anonymous World Services encouraged the development of intergroups around the world. Some intergroups had two meetings, and others had 100 meetings. Is this organization or chaos? To have proper, well laid out plans for induction, training, and participation require appropriate levels of organization. We are not to be organized. Nor are we to be examples of chaos. We have to find the balance in between. Usually, the best organization is that which is necessary to avoid chaos.

Moderators, Archivists, and Secretaries

In one period, the moderators for the phone bridge organized sufficiently to induct new moderators, to train them, and to consider appropriate moderator boundaries. In a subsequent period, different choices regarding the technology for moderating eliminated most of that organization structure as no longer needed. The role of the moderator and the anonymity of these trusted servants have also changed.

If we do not have World Service Committees that have secretaries to keep the minutes and archivists to gather that committee's pieces of our history, we will surely lose the continuity and momentum that we gain slowly. If we do not have group secretaries who maintain and pass on the results of group conscience, we often rework the same topics without needing to do so.

Let us be organized enough to accomplish our primary purpose: to carry the message to those who still suffer. That means that we need GSA communities to support groups, intergroups, and GSAWS with money, time, and service within the committees and the GSA World Services Conference.

Equality

Tradition Nine speaks to me of equality. We are all here in GSA to give freedom from compulsive eating. Everyone has earned a seat, and we are all one bite away from active addiction. I was not "managed," when I became a member. I was not "supervised." I saw a person with whom I identified, and I asked for help. I was lost and looking for direction. A person who spoke of freedom from food gave me some suggestions. Following the GreySheet food plan and taking suggestions uncovered my spirit. As the layers of pain, loss, anger, fear, secrecy, and lies melted, I found who I was and what my Higher Power wanted for me. I was one among many, and it felt like home. I knew a new freedom.

Rotating Leadership

GSA has a Board of Trustees with rotating leadership. There is not one person who governs. We follow principles, not personalities. Everyone has an equal voice and opportunities to be heard. We have service committees that keep our worldwide program unified via the WSC. Some are developing resources for GSA. I have my strengths and weaknesses, and service gives me opportunities for growth. When I know the term of service prior to volunteering, it makes service manageable. It's healthy to do service and then to let others have an opportunity to serve. I enjoy watching others in positions that I have held. I learn by observing how others deal with situations that challenged me. I am also a resource for them if they ask for my experience. I will be finishing my service terms this fall, and have begun to announce this at my local meetings. It is time to pass on the gift of service.

Tradition Nine Questions:

1. Why should the program refrain from organizing? What kind of 'organization' would be negative? Is 'oversight' or 'supervision' negative?
2. What are service boards or committees?
3. Under what circumstances can service boards or committees be formed?
4. What are the penalties of uncontrolled authority?
5. How can this tradition be demonstrated at home, in work relationships, or in other organizations?
6. Why refrain from authority and demanding behaviors in relationships in and out of the program? Why not?
7. Is the Board of Trustees bound by the same principles as members and groups?
8. What is incorporation?

Tradition Ten: GreySheeters Anonymous has no opinion on outside issues; hence the GSA name ought never be drawn into public controversy.

GSA as a whole has no opinion on outside issues. An individual group has no opinion on outside issues. An individual within the organization has no opinion as a member of GSA, but, of course, each has the right to his or her opinion. Our return to sanity includes a responsible lifestyle in which we vote, participate in religious organizations or other spiritual endeavors, accept community responsibilities, and in some cases, participate in political affairs at local, state, national, and global levels, if we wish to do so.

That means that the responsibilities of a GSA member are twofold. Within the organization of GSA, we express no opinion on outside issues, whatever they may be, while at the same time outside the organization of GSA we choose to be actively involved with the issues and causes we hold dear.

What are outside issues? One member defines outside issues as "anything that is outside of personal relationship with my abstinence and GSA recovery with steps, traditions, and concepts. If we engage in inventory taking of anyone except ourselves, we are involved in outside issues."

"Keeping my eyes on my plate" is the description another GSA member used to simplify Tradition Ten to its most basic tenet.

The Tenth Step and the Tenth Tradition go hand-in-hand. If we take personal daily inventories, the need to look at another person's inventory may be removed. Each one has enough to do dealing with one daily inventory. These are the joined elements of Step Ten and Tradition Ten.

When we work the steps, the need to comment on outside issues, becomes unnecessary. We hold no opinion on any outside issues, and we choose to refrain from drawing our GSA name into public controversy.

Our GSA community success and our abstinence depend upon the unique focus we share on compulsive eating and food addiction and the recovery of individuals with this disease through the practice of the steps, traditions, and concepts.

Tradition Ten Personal Experiences:

The GSA Food Plan

Cease and desist letters arrived for GreySheeters Anonymous. On one occasion, a letter addressed the issue of references on the GSA website. Another included the reference to the GreySheet food plan when we were attempting to copyright the pamphlet regarding the information on a solution for compulsive eaters and food addicts.

GSAWS had the opportunity to address the GreySheet food plan and to create one uniquely for GSAWS, Inc. A couple of members attempted it with surveys of the active literature and world service conference committees and those Board of Trustee members who were willing to participate in sharing what their abstinence included. The decision was instead to "fight." The process resolved into the negotiated sale of the GreySheet to GSAWS, Inc. The thousands in the cost of the GreySheet were small compared to the legal costs, however; the outcome is that GSAWS, Inc. now owns the rights to copy and distribute the GreySheet food plan. GSAWS now holds the responsibility to protect its copyright and trademark from unauthorized use.

Outside Issues

The outside issues in *other* organizations include use or abstinence from use of medications, the choice to have or not have phone bridge meetings, designation of sweeteners as an addiction or not, participation in World Services as GSRs or Intergroup Service Representatives or both, rotation of service in the World Service Structure, the use of coins to celebrate anniversaries, and finally literature associated with the individual organization or continuation of the use of another anonymous program's literature without creation of unique literature.

Safe Haven

GSA is my haven away from politics, finances, and world events. It is a place where my only focus is building a defense against the first bite. No one is campaigning for office or promoting personal endeavors. We avoid arguments between members by steering clear of these issues and by unifying in our common solution. My life experience has shaped me and my beliefs. Each person experiences life events in a personal way. Each has a unique reality. I honor my path and the paths of others by keeping my opinions quiet about topics not related to GSA. I need everyone's experience, strength and hope to contribute to my recovery. I love the feeling of belonging: of being in a room of people who have been where I have been with food and have learned a new way of life. We speak the same language.

If I were to spend time during a meeting talking about my political or religious beliefs, I would be sure to alienate group members. If I keep the focus on where I came from, how I got to GSA, and the life I have today, we stay on the common ground and support each other. We have no reason to speak harshly to each other. It's a relief that the GSA name won't be on the front page of the paper because we were involved in an investment scandal, we crossed a picket line, or we endorsed a candidate for office. None of that matters to us. In meetings, we have only one thing in mind, and our only agenda items are attaining and maintaining GreySheet abstinence and passing it on.

There are events in people's lives that increase their anxiety level, and they need to talk about going through the events without using food as a crutch. These are amazing "No Matter What's," and very important to share. Group members have shared that they received bad news and needed help. The GSA community rallies, and other members who have been through this can use their experiences to help their fellow traveler navigate this life altering event. People have dated, gotten married, honeymooned, divorced, been pregnant, given birth, lost children, lost spouses, lost a limb, lost a job, and lost a home. This is when our community shines. We come together as a support for our fellow and help in ways that are priceless. We listen. We are present. We weigh and measure our food and don't eat no matter what. We all have ups and downs, and we are all complex individuals, but when it comes to our GreySheet, it's the one common solution upon which we all agree.

Tradition Ten does not mean that members are not allowed to have opinions on outside issues, whatever the issues are. As GSA members, we don't give opinions on other issues. It would be easy for us to develop an opinion on how to treat eating disorders, or that the GS plan is best for everybody, or that a certain religious or political view is correct or wrong. But we don't do this as an organization, of course. I think this tradition is protecting us.

Tradition Ten Questions:

1. What is an opinion? How may I abstain from expressing my opinions when participating as a member of GSA?
2. What is an outside issue?
3. When I abstain from expressing my opinion on outside issues, how does this support GSA as a whole?
4. What is gossip? How can I abstain from gossiping?
5. Are there situations where sharing about another person's circumstances is not gossiping? When can it be positive? What makes the difference? Am I willing to respect the wishes of those who never want anyone to talk about them for any reason?
6. How are Step Ten and Tradition Ten related to each other?
7. What purpose does inventory taking serve?
8. How does public controversy interfere with abstinence?
9. How does abstinence from activities that would draw GSA into public controversy support abstinence?
10. What topics raise controversy?
11. What topics focus on abstinence?
12. How can we employ these concepts in our family life? At our work sites? In our communities? In these locations, what might be the outcomes of abstinent behaviors?
13. Some people use the acronym THINK (Thoughtful, Honest, Intelligent, Necessary, and Kind.) Others use the question 'How important is it anyway?' How could relationships improve by using these two techniques?
14. How else can I abstain from public controversy?

Tradition Eleven: Our public relations policy is based on attraction rather than promotion; we need always maintain personal anonymity at the level of press, radio, and films.

The foresight of our public relations policy in GSA began with our predecessor. The lessons learned were not ones we need to rediscover. It is easy to understand why compulsive eaters would be attracted to GSA when they see members lose significant amounts of weight. For instance, a 100-pound weight loss is noticeable, and many people want to know how it is possible. For members who have little or no weight change, the challenge of attraction is more subtle. Improved clarity of mind and serenity may not be so obvious to other people. When an opportunity arises to share, as so often happens when we are observed weighing and measuring our food, we rely on descriptions, photos, and our stories of experience, strength, and hope.

Members invited to share about GSA in a place that would potentially skyrocket our membership, like a published article, noted that the requirement for the particular offer was public face recognition of the interviewees. By respecting our Eleventh Tradition, the GreySheeters Anonymous members respectfully requested that our anonymity tradition be honored. No agreement, yet. In another location, TV coverage that respected the Eleventh Tradition provided information for potential new members of GSA.

No individual should ever become the public 'face' of GSA by allowing the press to display an image or full name. It would be too much responsibility for a member. Any misstep on the part of the individual might reflect poorly on GSA as a whole. This would be unfair to the rest of the membership. Print articles can be written about GSA without identifying individual members by full names, and interviews can be conducted with faces and voices obscured to prevent recognition.

This tradition relates to anonymity in the press, radio, and films. In private conversations, and web groups, many members share recipes, their writings on abstinence and recovery, and requests for experience, strength, and hope, regarding diverse topics such as dietary preparations for medical procedures, travel meals, and food for members training for endurance events. Other members respond to share specific examples of their experience, strength, and hope.

In the fellowship, members often identify themselves by first and last names in closed meetings. In this way, members know other members and how to reach them. Because of our promise of anonymity, we do not usually go up to other members we encounter in public places unless they are alone or have given us permission to do so. We do not share any phone numbers, other than our own, without permission. We abstain from discussing other members who are not present. We respect the anonymity of anyone in the program. We have the right to choose to disclose our membership, except when to do so would suggest without permission that someone else is a GSA member.

An aspect of GSA, similar in fact, to that of the experience of the founders of the first 12 step program, was the absence of an acknowledged medical model that supported complete abstinence from grain, sugar, and alcohol. Those nutritionists and doctors unfamiliar with the struggles of compulsive eaters and food addicts of our type believed that moderation in all dietary elements could work to relieve both weight and compulsion in the compulsive eater or food addict. Not so, based on our collective experience. As with other 12 step programs for addicts who abstain from their addictions, complete abstinence is the only solution for this addiction. Also, we weigh and measure and eat our food and no more or less as committed with our sponsor.

We as members of GSA have the opportunity regularly to share in a way that does not include press, radio, and films. Whenever one of us talks to a doctor, dentist, or any other health professional, we can share GSA literature and our personal recoveries in GSA. This is an opportunity to extend the information about GSA to the professionals.

Those with other eating problems have been able to eat differently; however, the stories that some share may describe the progressiveness of the disease. What some could eat earlier in their lives was no longer viable at a later time in life. Whether by the initial or progressive nature of the disease, those who found success in GSA were ones who were willing to go to any lengths to avoid the compulsions, cravings, hungers, delusions, and weight "yo-yo-ing."

Of course information is necessary to help people become attracted to GSA and to encourage interest in GSA. This information is on our website. After resolution of copyright issues, public information pamphlets have been distributed. Information can be published in the media. We offer information about GSA in public service announcements. With our permission and encouragement, friends and family may share with others the solution we have found. The experience, strength, and hope of those in the solution in GSA will always be our most effective means of attracting others.

Some members believe that nothing can be stated publicly about GreySheeters Anonymous. This is not accurate. Notices of meetings' local days and times placed in public media and on bulletin boards help carry the message. Some individuals may not want to be public in their use and declaration of the GSA program. Others regularly distribute to the curious the "*Can't Stop Eating*" wallet cards.

Tradition Eleven Personal Experiences:

Protection

Tradition Eleven protects everyone who walks into a GSA meeting. We are all protected. I feel very safe because of this Tradition. I am very open about my recovery in GSA, but I completely respect that others are not. It is not my business to expose or break any other member's anonymity. A GSA meeting is a sacred space, where we discuss our experience with food and how to deal with our drug three times a day. I honor our sacred space. We are all equal. We are compulsive eaters and together build our defenses against the first bite. It doesn't matter if one is a doctor, actor, sanitation worker, or banker; it's about freedom from sugars, flours, and grains. It's about weighing and measuring our food NO MATTER WHAT. What a relief! We have found this grace.

Anonymity and Attraction

By maintaining anonymity at the level of press, radio, and films, there is no 'spokesperson' for GSA. I misunderstood this Tradition in the beginning, because I thought it meant that we couldn't put a notice in a local newspaper, place posters on community bulletin boards with the dates and times for meetings in the area, or have an Information Meeting for the public. I know now that all of those activities are acceptable. It means, though, if I were to do an interview about GSA in the paper or on the radio, I could only identify myself by my first name. If I were doing an interview on TV, I would not show my face or give my full name. If I were a TV Talk Show host and had lost weight with the help of GSA, I would not name GSA. I would not promote GSA. It's a program of attraction. If I were the same Talk Show host and a friend or coworker approached me struggling with food, I would certainly share the basics of GSA and offer to take the newcomer to a meeting. The difference is that a person came to me struggling, knew I would understand and that I had been where s/he was emotionally and physically. That is very different than sending the message out unsolicited to a broad group of people.

Weighing and Measuring No Matter What

I have never been bothered by weighing and measuring my food in public places or restaurants. I have the luxury of back to back abstinence, and the majority of people in my life would think it very strange if I didn't weigh and measure. I'm kind to waiters and waitresses at restaurants, and I am a very good tipper. If I'm going to a restaurant I have never been to, I call the chef during a quiet time of day and explain what I need for food, and we agree on a meal. I bring backup, just in case, but have never had to use it. I give my wait-staff a note to give to the chef with everything written down that we discussed and a tip. It's been perfect every time. On a couple of occasions, the chef brought my meal out to be certain it was right. The people I've been dining with have always commented on how fresh and delicious my abstinent meal looks. I do this so others around me can see how manageable it is to follow the GreySheet. I bring gorgeous meals to work and eat my lunch with others. When I'm offered foods that are not abstinent, I simply say, 'No, thank you.' If the person is interested in why I don't eat things, s/he will ask me. Abstinence is the best choice I make at a meal! I love the bounty of foods and the freedom from the phenomenon of craving. I'm not ashamed of what I do with food. I'm not ashamed of my behavior today. I couldn't say the same when I was in my addiction.

World Service at Work

World Service maintains and reports on the Treasury balance and holds a regular World Service Conference. When the World Service Conference takes place, it serves my group and me by creating conference approved literature, by developing guidelines for public information and website improvement and maintenance, and by addressing rotation of service. My group helps support World Services by sending funds from our 7th Tradition after the group's financial obligations have been met. This money that is sent to World Service pays for expenses like the Parliamentarian and Transcriber that helped with the first WSC, the web consultant who builds a GSA website, and the accountant who reviews the GSA Treasury. All of these paid professionals are compensated with a fair wage for their work. Each job is investigated, and we develop a list of tasks or job descriptors. Committee members then contact and interview potential workers to perform the responsibilities and request a proposal for time and cost. The information is then brought to the Board and the appropriate committee(s), voted on, and the professional is hired for the job.

Celebrities

Tradition Eleven protects our fellowship. For example, if a celebrity came to GreySheet and had success and then talked about it on any media being enthusiastic, then relapsed and gained weight, the public might not see GSA as a solution. This is one way that this tradition protects us. We have to know that this is about personal anonymity on these levels. This tradition does not mean that among GreySheeters we never talk about personal things like where we live and what we do. It is about protection outside in the public. Some fellowships have spokespersons speak with the public media. We too can have a Board member who is not a GSA member speak to the media on our behalf.

Tradition Eleven Questions:

1. When movie stars or other famous people attend meetings, am I anxious to spread the news? What is the appropriate response?
2. Who has the right to anonymity and why?
3. What are the reasons to hold anonymity precious at the level of press, radio, and films?
4. How can I maintain anonymity at the level of press, radio, and film?
5. What is the difference between attraction and promotion?
6. Am I wearing my GreySheet abstinence in an attractive manner?
7. Who defines personal anonymity? How?

Tradition Twelve: Anonymity is the spiritual foundation of all our traditions, ever reminding us to place principles before personalities.

The spiritual bases of anonymity are sacrifice and humility. Sacrifice is letting go of name recognition and becoming, some say, "Just one of God's kids." We humbly give up our position in the society and any fame or notoriety. In an inverted triangle, the top position anyone can assume is regular membership in a GSA group or outpost. Humility is the recognition that anonymity is the essence and foundation of all our traditions. The spirit of anonymity maintains individual humility. To avoid breaks of anonymity at the level of press, radio, and films, members maintain the respect of the Twelfth Tradition. Our collective goal is to share the message: there is a solution for people who are compulsive eaters and food addicts. The message shared wears a cloak of public anonymity to maintain the security and trust of both newcomers and long-timers. Those who are famous, fearful, or fragile may wish to avoid public sharing of their recovery in GSA.

Some may find themselves more comfortable disclosing their membership after they accumulate lengthy periods of abstinence. Some regularly share with restaurant staff and others what they do and why. Some say remarkable things like, "I weigh and measure my food to be sure I eat enough food. I used to weigh 100 pounds more than I do now." Some members carry their photos from pre-abstinent days because "When sharing about GSA recovery, a picture is worth a 1000 words."

Whenever someone inquires about what we are doing while weighing and measuring, there is an open window of opportunity to plant seeds of information by sharing the message of recovery. Done without personal fanfare or recognition at the level of press, radio, and films, this is a desirable way to share the message. One member remarked, "I think everyone who asks about my weighing and measuring has a problem with food or knows someone who does. I go on to share the greysheet.org website and sometimes my phone number."

We are all free to disclose our membership in GSA. We can do this simply by acknowledging individually, one-on-one, "I am a member of GreySheeters Anonymous, a twelve-step program for people who suffer from the phenomenon of food craving. I weigh and measure three meals a day from the GreySheet. I commit them to my sponsor or another qualified person, and I do not eat between meals except for water, black coffee, tea, or diet soda." We can share the message.

The principles associated with the Twelve Steps are honesty, hope, faith, courage, integrity, willingness, humility, self-discipline, love for others, perseverance, spiritual awareness, and service. The principles of the Traditions include unity, trust, desire for abstinence, autonomy ("except in matters affecting other groups or GSA as a whole"), purpose, independence, self-support, non-professional (commonality among my fellows), creativity, freedom from controversy, attraction, and anonymity. When we put the principles we learned in the Twelve Steps and Twelve Traditions into practice we increase the harmony we experience with our fellows.

In GSA, there are many personalities. Since we wish to support our organization as it grows, we learn to place principles before personalities. We learn to give with love and service, to trust our trusted servants, and to be as honest, loving, and kind as we can be. By striving to demonstrate love and tolerance and to align our will with our Higher Power's will for us as individuals and as members of an organization, we practice application of these principles.

Tradition Twelve Personal Experiences:

Principles and Personalities

We all have principles and personalities, but here we have to keep the principles in mind. The problem is that we all have different interpretations of where we are with the principles. If there were no individuals with personalities that include traits such as perseverance, responsibility, love for fellow man, or continuing No Matter What, there would not be a GreySheeters Anonymous. So, we do need to have these personalities. In the process of working the program, we learn the principles that become embedded in our personalities and share them with our sponsees. Studying traditions and concepts and working the steps as best we can with both step and service sponsors are necessities and options for increased health and well-being.

Support Inside and Anonymity Outside

Anonymity works on the outside. Inside the GSA rooms, we have to know each other. We might ask about a person who is not present and perhaps hear that this person is not well and needs support. If we were completely anonymous, how could we help each other? This program is based on supporting each other.

I sit in GreySheet meetings and listen to members share intimate stories about their lives. I have become more emotionally vulnerable in my group than I am anywhere else. I am safe in the group. I am protected by Tradition Twelve. I know that if I run into fellow members in the community, they won't disclose or reference anything I shared in the meeting. It's a sacred space. I have emotionally matured because of this program. By allowing myself to heal with the help of my sponsor, my GSA group, and the Twelve Steps and Traditions, I am able to be of maximum service to others and to live with grace and humility, one among many.

A Change of Perception

When I was first abstinent, I would go to my meeting and listen to people share. In my head, I was judgmental toward them and their shares. I would assume that they didn't know what it was like to be abstinent and have no money to buy food. They were in normal sized bodies. How could they know the pain of being morbidly obese? I made assumptions. My friends in GSA pointed out that I might reflect on the parts of shares with which I identified and leave the rest. The longer I stayed, the more my judgments lessened and the more I was identifying with everyone. They all spoke 'my language.' They all were beaten up and broken when it came to food. They all wanted peace and freedom from the hell of compulsive eating. All of our outsides looked different, but our insides were very much the same. What a revelation it was!

I appreciate those coming to the meeting because I need their help to stay abstinent. I need to listen to them share their 'No Matter What' situations because one day I may be faced with a similar situation. We are all navigating our lives abstinently. There may be a time when I am in the middle of an emergency, and I may need to contact a member on my group phone list for help. I am confident in saying that I would help any member at any time, and they would do the same for me. We don't have to be friends, but we are supportive of each other.

Messengers

Our scales have sometimes served as a means to share the message of hope for food addicts. People ask, "What is that? Why are you weighing your food?" These are opportunities to serve as anonymous messengers.

Tradition Twelve Questions:

1. What is humility? How is it related to Tradition Twelve?
2. What is a sacrifice? How is it related to Tradition Twelve?
3. Where is anonymity for GSA individuals required in order to support the continuity and longevity of our program? Why?
4. In what circumstances may I 'break my anonymity?'
5. What are the principles that we place before personalities?
6. What are examples of the ways in which I apply principles before personalities?

A NEW BEGINNING

If you have read all of these pages and have answered all of these questions, you have completed one pass through the Steps and Traditions of GreySheeters Anonymous. For us, this is the beginning of a life-long process. With the assistance of your sponsor and fellow travelers in GreySheeters Anonymous, we hope that each finds what works and the freedom that we have experienced. During the next experience with these chapters, some choose a number of questions to answer in each or choose the questions that seem the most pertinent to the present moment. May you share what you find with those you sponsor and in the meetings you attend. May your changes as a result of working with these principles demonstrate the attraction that carries the message to another compulsive eater or food addict who still suffers inside or outside the rooms of GreySheeters Anonymous.

Some of us review the freedoms again. We will know freedoms beyond our wildest dreams:

- Freedom from the phenomenon of physical craving.
- Freedom to experience clarity of mind.
- Freedom to eat diversely from a wide variety of delicious and nourishing fruits, vegetables, oils/fats, and proteins.
- Freedom to live in a body healthier than any previously known.
- Freedom to become what each of us always wished to be or someone new.
- Freedom from the exorbitant cost, serious damage, and health consequences of food addiction and compulsive eating behaviors and thinking.
- Freedom to relate to others independently and interdependently.
- Freedom to experience one's own reality.
- Freedom to express oneself clearly and authentically to others and Higher Power.

- Freedom to set and keep appropriate external and internal boundaries, the ones that hold others at appropriate distances and those that contain what comes from inside oneself.
- Freedom to fulfill the potential ignored or forgotten and to become who I AM now.
- Freedom to strive to align with Higher Power's will.

Taking full responsibility for our actions in the past and present we walk forward in freedom.

We consider how to carry this message of recovery and hope to fulfill repeatedly our primary purpose: to stay abstinent and carry the message to others who still suffer. I am responsible. We are responsible. We have a solution for compulsive eaters and food addicts. It works. Let us share this fellowship and these steps and traditions with others who want to do what we do to have what we have. One day at a time... No Matter What. We place our food in one hand and life in the other, and we do NOT clap! Complete abstinence from our binge foods and other triggers is the solution.

Thank you for doing what we do ONE DAY AT A TIME NO MATTER WHAT.

The Call to Action: comments, new stories, or experiences can be submitted to: *literature@greysheet.org*

For more information about our program, please visit our website: *www.greysheet.org*

THE TWELVE STEPS*

1. We admitted we were powerless over food - that our lives had become unmanageable.
2. Came to believe that a Power greater than ourselves could restore us to sanity.
3. Made a decision to turn our will and our lives over to the care of God *as we understood Him.*
4. Made a searching and fearless moral inventory of ourselves.
5. Admitted to God, to ourselves, and to another human being the exact nature of our wrongs.
6. Were entirely ready to have God remove all these defects of character.
7. Humbly asked Him to remove our shortcomings.
8. Made a list of all persons we had harmed, and became willing to make amends to them all.
9. Made direct amends to such people wherever possible, except when to do so would injure them or others.
10. Continued to take personal inventory and when we were wrong promptly admitted it.
11. Sought through prayer and meditation to improve our conscious contact with God, *as we understood Him*, praying only for knowledge of His will for us and the power to carry that out.
12. Having had a spiritual awakening as the result of these Steps, we tried to carry this message to compulsive eaters, and to practice these principles in all our affairs.

* The Twelve Steps and Twelve Traditions of Alcoholics Anonymous have been reprinted and adapted with the permission of Alcoholics Anonymous World Services, Inc. ("A.A.W.S."). Permission to reprint and adapt this material does not mean that Alcoholics Anonymous is affiliated with this

program. A.A. is a program of recovery from alcoholism only - use of A.A.'s Steps, Traditions and Concepts or an adapted version in connection with programs and activities which are patterned after A.A., but which address other problems, or use in any other non-A.A. context, does not imply otherwise. 1. We admitted we were powerless over alcohol - that our lives had become unmanageable. 2. Came to believe that a Power greater than ourselves could restore us to sanity. 3. Made a decision to turn our will and our lives over to the care of God *as we understood Him*. 4. Made a searching and fearless moral inventory of ourselves. 5. Admitted to God, to ourselves, and to another human being the exact nature of our wrongs. 6. Were entirely ready to have God remove all these defects of character. 7. Humbly asked Him to remove our shortcomings. 8. Made a list of all persons we had harmed, and became willing to make amends to them all. 9. Made direct amends to such people wherever possible, except when to do so would injure them or others. 10. Continued to take personal inventory and when we were wrong promptly admitted it. 11. Sought through prayer and meditation to improve our conscious contact with God *as we understood Him*, praying only for knowledge of His will for us and the power to carry that out. 12. Having had a spiritual awakening as the result of these Steps, we tried to carry this message to alcoholics, and to practice these principles in all our affairs.

THE TWELVE TRADITIONS*

1. Our common welfare should come first; personal recovery depends upon GSA unity.
2. For our group purpose there is but one ultimate authority -- a loving God as He may express Himself in our group conscience. Our leaders are but trusted servants; they do not govern.
3. The only requirement for GSA membership is a desire to stop eating compulsively.
4. Each group should be autonomous except in matters affecting other groups or GSA as a whole.
5. Each group has but one primary purpose -- to carry its message to the compulsive eater who still suffers.
6. A GSA group ought never endorse, finance, or lend the GSA name to any related facility or outside enterprise, lest problems of money, property, and prestige divert us from our primary purpose.
7. Every GSA group ought to be fully self-supporting, declining outside contributions.
8. GreySheeters Anonymous should remain forever nonprofessional, but our service centers may employ special workers.
9. GSA, as such, ought never be organized; but we may create service boards or committees directly responsible to those they serve.
10. GreySheeters Anonymous has no opinion on outside issues; hence the GSA name ought never be drawn into public controversy.
11. Our public relations policy is based on attraction rather than promotion; we need always maintain personal anonymity at the level of press, radio, and films.
12. Anonymity is the spiritual foundation of all our Traditions, ever reminding us to place principles before personalities.

* The Twelve Steps and Twelve Traditions of Alcoholics Anonymous have been reprinted and adapted with the permission of Alcoholics Anonymous World Services, Inc. ("A.A.W.S."). Permission to reprint and adapt this material does not mean that Alcoholics Anonymous is affiliated with this program. A.A. is a program of recovery from alcoholism only - use of A.A.'s Steps, Traditions and Concepts or an adapted version in connection with programs and activities which are patterned after A.A., but which address other problems, or use in any other non-A.A. context, does not imply otherwise. 1. Our common welfare should come first; personal recovery depends upon A.A. unity. 2. For our group purpose there is but one ultimate authority—a loving God as He may express Himself in our group conscience. Our leaders are but trusted servants; they do not govern. 3. The only requirement for A.A. membership is a desire to stop drinking. 4. Each group should be autonomous except in matters affecting other groups or A.A. as a whole. 5. Each group has but one primary purpose—to carry its message to the alcoholic who still suffers. 6. An A.A. group ought never endorse, finance, or lend the A.A. name to any related facility or outside enterprise, lest problems of money, property, and prestige divert us from our primary purpose. 7. Every A.A. group ought to be fully self-supporting, declining outside contributions. 8. Alcoholics Anonymous should remain forever nonprofessional, but our service centers may employ special workers. 9. A.A., as such, ought never be organized; but we may create service boards or committees directly responsible to those they serve. 10. Alcoholics Anonymous has no opinion on outside issues; hence the A.A. name ought never be drawn into public controversy. 11. Our public relations policy is based on attraction rather than promotion; we need always maintain personal anonymity at the level of press, radio, and films. 12. Anonymity is the spiritual foundation of all our Traditions, ever reminding us to place principles before personalities.